BROTHERS OF THE STATE

BROTHERS OF THE STATE

DARRELL LACEY

EBook ISBN: 978-1-958783-02-3
Trade Paperback ISBN: 978-1-958783-01-6
Hardcover ISBN: 978-1-958783-00-9
Cover design by Jasmine Butcher
Cover artwork image by RealCreation
Published by Ozark Hollow Press
PO Box 4573
Joplin, Missouri 64803
Lia Wu, Publisher
Ozark Hollow Press Edition 2022
Printed in the USA

CONTENTS

FOREWORD

There are many reasons I want to write this foreword for *Brothers of the State*. I am a child who experienced abuse. I was in the foster care system. I live in their home community and know the family because we were close in age. My passion and life's work is about helping families to avoid this pattern or recover from the trauma. Most importantly, it matters that this story is heard. The courage to tell the story is an agreement with self that you are strong enough and you will be okay.

Confronting your story requires you to relive pieces and parts of events that you once experienced–and changed you. The re-telling, especially after not being heard or helped, is both courageous and challenging. To defy the anger and pain and keep it from immersing you again is bold, powerful, and great. As you read Darrell's words, may you find the courage to be a good person, good parent, good brother, good human so that others are spared the hurt that buries itself in your soul. It never goes away, only shifts.

I am a survivor. Abuse touched my life deeply. It changed me. Reading this story fuels me. The pain pursued me for years until I decided to make it my purpose. I turned my pain into my passion. I healed and now work as a therapist helping others avoid the lack that becomes abuse. I encourage others to face their trauma head on and change their path. That's where the POWER is.

As Darrell touches your heart, let it be known that your every action matters—they stick. And, the only way to recover is: practice.

Sandra Main
Possibility Junction

For my brothers

CHAPTER ONE

My oldest brother, John, lives two hours away. He always calls me to ask stupid questions.

"Have you ever seen a ghost?"

My answer is always the same. "You know I don't buy into that bullshit, John."

"Where's the first place you'd go if you went back home?"

"Why would I go there, John?"

"It's your hometown man, show the loyalty."

He always rambles on how Deramus Park would be his first stop, followed by Mom's grave.

He always wraps the call up with, "I'd go back to Smelter Street and dig a red brick from the sidewalk before they remove them and try to erase history."

Uneven brick sidewalks have been smooth cement almost a decade and a half, unknown to him. Our family says he's just nostalgic, an old soul. I know it's because he's agoraphobic, suffering from debilitating panic attacks.

Every time he slides behind the wheel of his truck to make the drive back home, he navigates his way to the exit, leaving Kansas City, Kansas. Every time he ends up pulling to the side of the road, placing the truck in park, on the verge of passing out. His trembling hands reach in his glove compartment, seeking his ever-faithful traveling companion, a brown paper bag. Every time.

He hyperventilates into it. Every time.

As the oxygen to carbon dioxide requirements thwart his agoraphobic prison, John composes himself to a point he feels he can drive. Looping around to the north exit, he heads back to Kansas City, frustrated, and defeated again. Every time.

But not this time.

Tonight, his call is unique.

Sure, he asks me where I'd go, what I'd do, if I see ghosts. I give the same answers I always do, but tonight he clarifies that he's not going home ever again.

He's made these threats before, but the insane rambling and elevated levels of screaming, accompanied by threats toward me and anyone who tries to stop him is new and to be taken seriously. "Fuck you!" he shouts down the line. Then, he mutters a beaten-down, "I'm done, bro... I am *done*!"

The phone goes dead, and he's not answering, so here we go, 2:30 in the morning and I'm driving down this familiar farm road for the first time since God knows how long, hating every mile, padding the odometer.

The cherry on the shit sundae?

A spring storm, tornado alley. Elevated winds, heavy rain, and sometimes sizable spheres of hail are rocking and rolling my ass all over the road, impeding me.

Visibility is shit and this road, Kellogg Road, is ripe for flash flooding if the ground is dry and compacted.

It's been dry for weeks now.

Fuck it. Let the flood waters come. That'll put a stop to this bullshit. It'll wash everything away. Maybe drown him and me and–

"Stop!" I yell aloud. *Pay attention to the road and keep your mind on getting there to stop his unstable ass.*

To make matters worse? In my mad dash out the door, I forgot my phone. I can picture that little rectangular bastard right now, nestled in the folds of my comforter on my queen-size bed where I left it in my rush, illuminating the fluffy pillow covered by a clean white cotton case where I'd been sleeping. Mocking me.

It takes an hour and a half to drive what should've taken fifty minutes. John's truck is there, a black Dodge Ram V-10. A regular gas guzzler if ever there was one.

"The damn thing gets ten miles to the gallon, bro, but it'll pull your house right off its foundation," he'd bragged. It'd been one of his good days.

It's still raining when I pull up beside John's monster of a truck. The accompanying electrical storm is putting on one hell of a show. Against the modern and dramatic backdrop, the two-story white farmhouse looks the same, faded and in need of a fresh coat of paint.

Some things never change. Unless somebody paints it for his lazy ass, it just isn't getting done. The old man always loved his free labor. I kill the lights, turn into the gravel drive and push the floor shifter to neutral, cutting the engine. As I get out, a bright flash illuminates the farm, followed by an ear-splitting boom.

"Jesus, that was close!" *Goddamn lightning.*

Making the walk up to the edge of the yard where the grass starts, I step onto the concrete pavers leading to the front porch. I push the screen door back. The front door is a quarter of the way open. A bright yellow flash fills the large living room window, and a simultaneous explosion halts my forward movement.

Too late, fucking rain. I didn't make it in time. Shit!

"Pweash, pweash."

It's muffled and gargled, but I know what I'm hearing, and it's not good.

"John, it's me. I'm coming in, okay?"

No answer.

I place my left hand on the frosted glass window, decorating the door. "It's me, bro. You hear me?"

At first there's nothing and then, in a dispassionate low voice, "It's over."

There's enough space between door and jamb to lean forward and audit the scene before popping my head back. *Shit, he's fucked. Nobody can help him now. Nobody.*

"Okay, I'm coming in, man."

I push the door and it creaks open and bumps the rubber stop, bouncing back toward me to rest against my shoulder.

"Hep me, pweash," the old man begs.

He had collapsed on the second step at the foot of the narrow stair-case that leads to the second story. A low-watt sconce on the living room wall proves enough light to see the blast took out his left eye, cheek, and most of the left side of his face right down to the molars. Rivulets of bright red blood are pooling on his neck and soaking his white tank top. From the looks of the dripping red splatter about six feet up on the wall, it happened at the foot of the stairs while he was still standing upright.

I feel the familiar sting in my eyes from a need to let loose a few tears. Not like at a wedding or joyous moment. It's the kind brought on by pent-up sadness or anger. I advance a few steps, making sure I can hightail it out of there fast should John go full on bonkers and decide two is better than one.

Blue acrid smoke hangs over the geezer's body.

"Pweash," he begs.

"Shhh, don't talk, man, you're going to make it worse," I say.

His right eye, a now companionless, functioning ice-blue, rolls in its socket, frantic.

The sound of gun metal and wood sliding backward and forward diverts my attention as John racks another shell into the receiver, letting the shotgun dangle in his right hand, barrel pointed at the floor.

"Easy, brother, be cool," I say.

His eyes stay focused on the overweight man he'd placed in this criti-cal, desperate state.

"It needed done, man. It was time. Way overdue, Joseph."

He pauses a moment, cocking his head left, an inquisitive look on his face. He appears to be studying his handiwork with the 12 gauge or, with any luck, realizing that he fucked up.

Whimpering, but not speaking, the man brings his trembling right hand up to his forehead, fingers palpating his left eye socket. His lone, widowed right eye widens in horror, realizing its once present and func-tional mate is no more. The sobbing grows.

"Crybaby," John growls. "I thought you were tough, raised by a real badass." He shakes his head.

The obese man turns his head to the right. Blood, in steady streams, snake down his neck, folds of fat creating separate and new avenues of travel.

Then, my brother lets out a one word scream loud enough to have me looking for the exit.

"HA!"

He's pointing with his left index finger at the man's crotch. Forming before my eyes, right in the middle of the old man's striped, beige and blue pajama bottoms, is a darkening patch of wetness. The man is bawling. Shamed by what is happening to him as John stands pointing almost gleefully.

"Come on, John. He's dying, man."

The smile disappears from my brother's face, replaced with disgust.

"Not yet, bro, not yet."

John brings the shotgun up to his chest and I brace for the loud report to come. Instead, he pulls his right, boot-clad foot back and, with one large step forward, drills the man in the ribs.

The man lets out an abrupt "oof" and sucks for air without luck. John hammers him again and again. The man, desperate for precious oxygen, curls up–diaphragm frozen in place–and rolls onto his right side. John kicks again, aiming for the tailbone.

"Pissant!" John hollers. His foot races forward, this time connecting square on his victim's lower back. "You fucking sinner!"

With a shuddering sob, the man squeaks out, "Pweash, schtop, pweash."

Attempting to disarm my brother or reason him away from the man crosses my mind.

Could I jump him?

Maybe so, maybe not. This has been building for decades and when John's candle is lit, you better believe somebody's going to see the light. Once my oldest brother's mind is made up, that's all she wrote. However, this overjoyed human being torturing the man at the foot of the stairs is not my brother. If I mess with him, I may join that man on the floor.

Didn't he have it coming?

Didn't he?

Part of me, deep down inside where a person taps into the animalistic part of their soul, wanted to join John. Longed to have a hand in making this man's last moments as painful and as terrifying as possible.

A wisp of fabric at the top of the stairs snaps me back to my world, filled with rational people and thoughts. John, now pointing the gun at the man again, hasn't noticed her. God knows what damage he'll drop on her at this point. I widen my eyes, staring at her.

I assume this large woman sporting a nightgown resembling a pup tent is his better half. Terrified, I jerk my head to the right, egging her on to hightail it back into the shadows. Her petrified eyes meet mine. Her plump lips purse and she backs away into the darkness, understanding and fearing her movement might alert the wicked man with the shotgun to her presence.

As she dissolves into obscurity, I notice a phone in her hands. A land-line phone. The kind most folks don't have installed in their homes thanks to the convenience of cellular service. She's called for help or dialed 911 without speaking, alerting emergency services that something's amiss at the old farm on Kellogg Road.

Reasoning with my brother seems to be the best avenue right about then, so I begin, "John, you can still get out of this, man." It sounds like bullshit the second after I say it, and he knows it.

"No turning back now, brother," he whispers.

"You can run, man, just take off and disappear or even turn yourself in," I say.

For a sliver of a second, I can see I have him thinking. He stares at me, all the while pointing his shotgun at the man's neck, index finger ignoring the trigger discipline he'd learned in the army.

His brown eyes soften and for the first time since our mother passed away, fifteen years ago, a single tear slides down his left cheek. "He deserves this, and you know it," he croaks.

He regards the man, who at this point has rolled onto his back again. *Listen to him. Listen to your younger brother, for God's sake,* his one good eye pleads.

The sound of crunching, wet gravel reveals the authorities have arrived. More than one vehicle, gauging by the silent but many red and blue lights flooding the living room.

My brother looks at me and gives a small, tired smile. "Too late, bro... too late." Whatever snippet of a chance I thought I had to coerce him into running for the hills?

Gone.

Sure, he'd be a fugitive, but at least he'd be alive.

"You could give up and tell them why," I plead.

He levels the barrel of the shotgun off and rests the end on the man's bobbing Adam's apple. Footsteps and disjointed talk drift through the half-open door. I drop to my knees and raise my hands in the air with my back to the authorities.

"We did, and they ignored us, goddamn it! So, it's their fault!"

His voice trails off, almost like a hushed whisper. "You tell them, Joseph, I'm tired."

His grimace softens again as he turns his attention to the overweight, bleeding lump on the floor. As he does, the man, almost mimicking me, raises his trembling right arm to the top of his head, giving up.

The police officer's voices become louder; their footfalls come faster, heading up the walk. Over the building noise, I still hear John's voice, loud and clear, saying like a prayer, "Burn in hell, demon, burn in hell." He presses the barrel deeper into the doughy flesh of the man's neck.

A lone, azure eye turns defiant and glaring, hateful. A familiar look.

"You're a shinner, you're a shinner!" the man cries.

"And you're the DEVIL!" John screams, jerking the trigger.

A white flash. The man's head parts from his torso—carotid arteries spurting the tacky, hot oil of life across the stairs, baseboards, and paneling.

John tosses the shotgun to his right.

Screams of a terrified loved one upstairs accompany my oldest brother as he drops to the floor, laying out spread eagle, face down.

Three police officers rush past me, guns drawn. The living room becomes ablaze with white flashlights mixing with red-and-blue pulses from their cruisers. A terrible mixture of crimson and sapphire reflected in pictures.

Pictures hung perfect, with painstaking and calculated care, on the devil's walls.

CHAPTER TWO

H ey, buddy! Come out from under there."
     When I opened my eyes, the reddish, orange haze through my lids turned brilliant white. The flashlight swung left, revealing red-and-blue flashing orbs. The sheer curtains of our living room creating a kaleidoscope of imminent foreboding.

A large hand reached for me. The man grabbed me by my t-shirt and yanked me out from under the couch with one easy pull. I had been sleeping... hiding... praying.

The officer planted me on unsteady feet and led me from the darkened living room, past the dilapidated staircase that led to the second story of The Mansion. He swung the busted screen door open, and we took two steps down the concrete stairs, walking to his cruiser, the policeman's hand still looped through my old, faded tee at the shoulder. He opened the door, told me to watch my head, and swept me into the back of his car.

He never frisked me, cuffed me, or read me my rights. Why would he? I had done nothing wrong. I was six years old. I was hiding under that smelly, piece-of-shit couch. Not from a thief, a killer, a monster, or things that go bump in the night. I was hiding from my mother.

There were some extenuating circumstances with our parents that took place the night they had removed my siblings and me.

It was lean times for our family and most other families we grew up around in the Midwest. We were poor, but hell, I didn't know we were. I was a kid and unaware of social status or earning capacity.

I remember the first time I realized there just wasn't enough. One evening, our dad was driving OTR in big rigs for a local company and was absent. Our mother sat us down for brown beans and rice. She encouraged us to finish everything in front of us. She collected the plates from all five kids and took them to the kitchen countertop. There, she had her dinner. The scraps we five kids had not eaten.

I also remember the never-ending game of hide-and-seek from the man who worked for the power company and would show up to turn off the electricity. The game continued with the representatives from the gas company and water department.

Most of our clothes came from the Church of Christ. It was like Christmas when they would show up with a big box of clothing. Sometimes, care packages of food and basic toiletries as well.

Our dad was a hard-working man and, sometimes, a hard-drinking man with a knack for cutting loose on certain weekend nights. Whether he did it because of an addiction, or he felt he deserved it after a hard day's work, I am not privy. This man took care of a wife and five kids on a paycheck that would average sixty bucks a week. He earned every penny. Every penny! If he wanted a drink on Friday night after a hard week's worth of work, then to hell with it.

I recall on a couple of occasions how the police would pull up at night, bringing him to the door after he'd gotten a snoot-full and destroyed the interior of a local watering-hole. They'd tell Mom, "Don't let him leave, because if he does and we catch him, he's getting locked up." She would thank them and do her part to shuffle Dad off to bed.

Mom and Dad had plenty of screaming matches and a few physical encounters. Dad weighed about two hundred and forty pounds. Mom about one hundred and ten, if that. By physical encounters, I mean it was as simple as Dad grabbing hold of Mom and placing her wherever he saw fit, never violent. I never witnessed him physically abuse our mom. He'd take hold of her and place her in a chair most of the time, trying to calm her down.

A doctor I am not, so I do not know, nor claim to know, the mental workings or the capacity of the human brain to take or endure a volatile situation before something goes haywire upstairs. Still, growing up, I became very aware—intimate even—with mental illness. As long as I could remember, my mother had been loosely diagnosed with a mental condition and prescribed medication—for all the good it did—to combat her "going". That's what we called it.

Going.

Two years before our ride in the constable's car, an incident took place with our mother that is, more or less, our first memory of her "going". She sat us down to that evening's dinner of pancakes and in silence tended to her business, placing the hotcakes in front of each of us and taking Dad his plate in the living room, not speaking at all. Not one peep.

She fed us, walked out of the kitchen, found her way to the bathroom, and cut her wrists. It was only minutes before Dad discovered her and had her in his arms, hauling ass out the front door, yelling back to our sister, the eldest sibling, Jennifer, to watch the baby, Julie, our youngest sibling.

As for why she did this, I do not know. Was it postpartum depression? A chemical imbalance from the meds she was always on? Perhaps the thought of having five kids and seeing no light at the end of the tunnel? I'm not sure. But seeing your father, a mountain of a man, with fear in his eyes, moving faster than you ever had and your mother, cradled in his arms with blood streaming from her wrists and blossoming into the front of his shirt leaves one hell of a mental picture burned into your thoughts.

Mom was admitted to the hospital for a brief spell. While she was recovering, her mother, our grandmother, stayed at the house and took care of us kids. She was a hot-tempered four-foot, ten-inch Hungarian hurricane we called Gigi. She loved us all, but she kept a tight leash to keep us in line. Gigi would have to stay with us during several instances when Mom had these episodes. I always associated Gigi with good food. She could cook! She passed that onto Mom, and Mom to all of us.

Another instance later on happened around the same kitchen table.

Mom, brooding and silent, trudged, almost machine-like, around the table, placing bowls of hot, steamy soup in front of each of us except the baby. Julie in her highchair and Mom's soup distribution complete, she seated herself at the head of the table and stared straight forward between all of us, my brothers and older sister, Jennifer, at the opposite end of the table, eyes searing. I'd bet money they felt as though Mom was burning a hole straight through them.

Four out of five of us kids had grown accustomed rather fast to subtle signs that she was checking out.

Going.

Jet black, mid-back length hair, neat, clean and always in place, whether at home or away, now hung down, obscuring her beautiful face. She would start carrying a brush around, jammed deep down into her back pocket, always at the ready, brushing, brushing. Sparkling, dark brown, almond-shaped eyes had transformed overnight into dull, lost, and distant orbs. She remained almost catatonic for several minutes. No finger-tapping. No blinking. Not a twitch. Then... BANG!

In an instant, dead eyes came to life. Pursed lips revealed teeth clenched tight. She shot bolt upright, opened her mouth, and screamed at the top of her lungs.

No words, just a solid, extended, ear-splitting, primal scream. With all of us in shock and the baby crying, startled by the loud eruption, she placed both hands under the edge of the kitchen table and lifted her end chest-high.

Hot tomato soup, bowls, spoons, and toast slid from her end, past me—bless the saints—and found their targets: my brothers and sister at the other end of the table. Baby still crying and two-thirds of the children covered in hot soup and crying, Mom slammed her end of the table back down. All the while, her deafening scream faded to a low growl.

Her eyes wet and blank, her face pallid and white, mouth snapped shut. She snatched the brush from her back pocket, turned on one heel, her back to us and the mess created, and walked away from her children, disappearing into the darkened living room off the kitchen.

Brushing, brushing... goddamn brushing.

Another unsettling incident took place one summer I did not witness, but seemed to shake my older brother, John, when he told the story to me in adulthood. We lived across the street from Washington Elementary School, which we all, except the youngest, attended. It was a one-story, red brick with white trim building lined on the west side with well-manicured hedge bushes. Sometimes we children would find a spot behind the hedges to play with a toy car or to dig in the rich, black soil surrounding the base of each shrub, much to the chagrin of the old custodian.

On this occasion, John was alone, seated behind the hedges that was facing across the street with a side view of our front door. It was a brilliant, sunny day.

"I was digging holes," John had said.

None of us really believed him. We boys were notorious for stealing Ken and Barbie figures from Jennifer. We'd place them in compromising positions, leaving them naked in their soil-covered shame to be found by their pissed off owner.

"I heard the front door to the Mansion creak open," he'd stated. "Mom stepped out the front door and down two steps to the concrete stoop. She walked to the middle of the small front yard, stopped, and held her hands out to her sides and her face pointed skyward, as though she were about to take flight.

"Then, she lowered her arms back to her sides and her face straight ahead. She turned to the left and walked toward the elm tree that grew on the east side of our home. When she reached the tree, she brought her arms straight out in front of her, opened them wide, took one step straight forward, and wrapped her arms around the tree as far around as they could reach."

At first, John thought she was giving the tree a hug. But then she bent her knees and pulled upward on her toes, trying to uproot this large tree out of the earth. After several more attempts, her arms scraped and bleeding, she let go of the elm tree and took one step backward.

He continued.

"Doing an about face, almost as disciplined as a soldier doing drill and ceremony, she trudged toward the same side of the house until she reached the crumbling particle board siding and stopped. Again, eyes gazing upward, arms outstretched, she stood in silence for several minutes."

It was then he explained, just as she had attempted with the tree, head now down and arms reaching groundward, she grasped the pipes that ran on each side of the forest-green gas meter and pulled her body as hard as she could muster, trying to dislodge the meter from its secure base.

After several more failed attempts, she gave up and, just as she had done before, pulled the old about face and with noble purpose walked to the center of the front yard and raised her head skyward, arms horizontal to the ground with palms up. Another couple of minutes passed with Mom standing statue still. Then—About face! Forward... March!... to the stoop, up the steps, through the creaky front door and back into the Mansion.

John isn't sure why this event has remained as one of the creepier moments out of the many that occurred. Maybe it was the fact that he was alone and the only child seeing it take place. Or maybe it's because when she marched toward the tree, he swears her eyes had locked to his even though he was obscured by the thick hedge that provided his cover.

Over the next few weeks, the instability in our home increased. Our mom had more "going" moments and our dad began hanging out at a bar after work instead of coming straight home. When he'd arrive back at the Mansion after putting away some of Lynchburg, Tennessee's finest, it would almost always lead to a shouting match between the two of them. After a few arguments, Mom started locking the door by supper time.

"Open this goddamn door, Evie. You open this goddamn door, right goddamn now."

He'd knock and holler out minor threats for a bit and then take off to God knew where until he sobered up. The next day after work, Dad would show up at dinner and, if Mom was in her right frame of mind, they'd act as though nothing had happened the night before. He'd make up songs about how great of a cook she was and she would call him "pumpkin".

These events played out a few more times with her checking out more often and him drunker and angrier each time. Mom began making John hide under her and Dad's bed with the telephone on these nights. She had devised a plan.

If Dad came home inebriated and pissed off, John was to be dressed in the darkest clothing he owned. Should Dad make it into the house and put his hands on her, John was to call the police, leave the phone out of its cradle, and snake his way out from under the bed. Further instructions from Mom had him crawl out of their room and down the stairs into the basement. The plan would culminate with John climbing through a ground-level window, hauling ass to the neighbors' house, and asking them for help.

On one particular evening, Dad was absent again, pickin'em up and puttin'em down at a bar. John put on his darkened clothes at bedtime and took up his position as he had been doing for a couple of weeks. Dad found his way home and began his drunken pleading while raining thunderous blows on the door. This night, things got out of hand. He seemed more pissed than the other times.

Dad was a large, powerful man. He was what one might call a "force of nature". A woman I worked with later in life, Brenda, told me a story about him. She and her husband owned the bar that our dad frequented.

She said, "Your father would come in, skin basted bronze from the sun, his hair thick, blond, and wavy. Just a real good-looking man. Once he started downing the brown liquor, he would tear the bar and anyone foolish enough attempting to stop him apart. Not to mention, almost every table and chair in our establishment had to be replaced."

Well, that was the man who showed up that night at our home. After being ignored by his wife and children, he bashed his way through the door and was standing over our mom in mere moments. John said Dad was leaning over the bed and talking to Mom in a voice he'd never recalled hearing come from our dad. He accused her of cheating on him and berated her awful. He said things no son should hear a father say to his mother.

Ever.

After a few parting words, Dad turned and walked out of the bedroom and left the house with Mom crying, John still under the bed, phone still in its cradle, and wood splintered from the front door swimming in his wake. Things were becoming worse by the week at the old Mansion.

Sometimes when Mom would "go", she would call her mother, our grandma Gigi, if the phone bill had been paid. Mom would argue with Gigi about bad people trying to get us. Gigi would counter and tell her she needed help, and that she was on her way over to make sure we were alright. Mom would accuse her of being one of the evil people or of being a witch.

Gigi would hang up on Mom and head our way. After Mom would hang up the phone, she would turn to us children, ordering one of us to go upstairs and get four bars of ivory soap.

Mom would say, "Spread out! Draw crosses on the windows. Go! Don't forget upstairs."

In her mind, this would ward off Gigi, and anyone else she suspected represented Satan. I half expected to see Gigi arrive on her kitchen broom, black hat and cloak fluttering behind her like the Wicked Witch of the West. Gigi would make it to our house and after some time could convince our mom she was her daughter's keeper, not the devil himself.

"You need help, Evie," she'd say.

Mom would calm down after a while and Gigi would schedule arrangements with her employer so she could watch us children.

Incidents such as these involving our mother and father lasted two years. There were other dates off and on in which my mom had a few more check outs. These were a few of the more memorable moments that remain seared in the folds of our gray matter. My childhood wasn't filled with Mom in a constant state of being "zoned out" or Dad in bars raising hell. On a lighter note, a deacon from our church visited our home attempting to prove he was just like our dad. This poor fella sits down and begins trying to emulate the perception he had of our dad. "You know, I'm just like you, big guy. I drink a cold beer and even enjoy a Playboy magazine now and then."

Dad told him to get the hell out of his house. "I don't allow that goddamn filth around these kids." My brothers and I laughed our asses off over that incident.

We had wonderful times as a family, going to church (minus Dad) or listening to music, playing kick-the-can or red rover with the neighborhood kids. We'd visit the school playground and climb the monkey bars or swing as high as we could on rows of swing-sets until the streetlights came on at dusk. We'd head home and, like clockwork, Mom had made something to eat out of nothing.

She loved us with all her heart, as did our dad. Their affection for each one of us could fill you with absolute joy. When a child not only knows but feels loved, he forgets the tough times. We may not have been secure in a monetary manner or have the nice things most people desire, but we had each other though.

Damned if we didn't feel like the Rockefeller's.

CHAPTER THREE

Then came the day that changed everything. Mom had checked out a day or two before. It started with the familiar brush in her back pocket, then the constant brushing of her not-so-tidy hair. It built into the vacant and lost look in her eyes and on her face. That grew into pacing, back and forth from living room to kitchen. The usual visual clues had a way of putting us on edge and filling us with dread, knowing she was "going".

It was a Friday. Dad's payday. Most of the wives or significant others of the men employed by the trucking company lined up after lunch at the main office and waited for the pay their men busted their asses for all week. Back at the Mansion, us four school-aged children were all home.

Mom, frantic, had awakened us that morning to inform us that we wouldn't be attending school because men, sinful men, were watching and waiting to take one, if not all of us, should we venture outside.

The school was across the street from our home. How the hell was anyone going to scoop up five children in less than a casual jaunt across the blacktop? None of us asked, though. We had learned early on not to press our mother during these episodes. So, we had settled in for a long day at home.

I had perched myself at a downstairs window, observing my class-mates and many others make their way down frost-covered sidewalks, safe and sound. I listened to the first bell ringing through a thin pane of glass and watched all the kids, crossing guards, and teachers as they went about their day. I didn't see any children screaming or running for their lives. The crossing guard didn't turn into a demon and the evil men must have kept to themselves hidden God knew where, waiting for their intended targets, because they never came to be. Once I knew everyone made it safe and sound inside the walls of the school, I headed into the kitchen to find something to eat. John stopped me and said, "Don't bother."

He opened the cereal and poured the contents into his bowl. Roaches poured out of the box and into the bowl, energetic and scurrying for cover of darkness after being disturbed.

I walked toward the doorway of the kitchen and stopped, horrified at what I was seeing. Mom was sitting at the table, flicking, flicking, flicking roaches to the floor, one at a time. Her right hand rested on the edge of the table and, as one of the filthy little bastards scrabbled within proper distance, she unwound her coiled index finger and flicked it to the floor. After sending one a few feet across the kitchen, she focused her desperate, dark eyes on me, not raising her head.

Her lips curled upward, and she asked in a whisper, "You wanna play?"

Her head bobbed up and down with accompanied soft, steady giggling. I didn't say a word. I backed out. I made my way to the couch and squeezed in between John and Jason, spooked as all get out.

It wasn't long after, Mom made her way to the living room and stood before us, eyes darting back and forth from one child to the next. Much like the march John had described when observing from the schoolyard hedges, she wheeled around on one foot and began marching back and forth, living room to bedroom and back. She repeated this for what must have been around an hour, silent, brushing, brushing, brushing.

After her last trip from the bedroom to the living room, she came to an abrupt halt and faced us. This woman who stood before us was our mom, but she wasn't. She was somewhere else, checked out and long gone. The way her icy stare bore through us, inspected us, was terrifying.

"Line up in a row! Now!" she roared.

We jumped to it with frightened rigidity.

"No. No! Noooo!" she bellowed. "Oldest to youngest!"

Doing our best to get it right as to not anger her any further, we moved as fast as possible, jostling into one another.

Then, in a much calmer tone, she told us we were to place our hands straight out in front of us and have our palms facing up.

I was more than confused and scared shitless, but I followed her commands. Mom began that slow march she had been doing, only this time it was from living room to kitchen, back and forth, brushing and mumbling. While she made her way to the kitchen again, Jennifer, who had edged her way into the living room from upstairs, said, "If she blows up, run!"

She could tell as well as the rest of us, if not better than us, that Mom wasn't here anymore.

Mom made her last back-and-forth trip and stopped by the end table next to that shitty couch. She reached down and plucked up the family Bible, settling her attention back on us. She paced back and forth, pausing in front of each of us. After several rounds of this odd ceremony, it appeared she'd concluded the family Bible would belong to Jason. She placed the good book on Jason's outstretched palms, as though it were tiffany crystal, then raised her left arm horizontal to the floor and pointed off toward her and Dad's bedroom.

"Go," she said.

Jason just stared up at her, confused and silent.

"Go!" she bellowed.

Jason slunk off toward the bedroom and she followed. The rest of us inched toward the doorway opening, watching to see what would become of our brother. She stopped him by the closet door and had him turn toward her, Bible still balanced on his palms.

"You have the devil's eyes," she said.

Jason, motionless, stared straight forward.

"Ice-blue eyes. Like your father... like the devil."

I couldn't have been happier to have dark brown eyes.

A loud crack echoed through the house, and the Bible fell to the floor. She had slapped him. The following silence was louder than the act itself. She had never, ever placed a hand on any of us, ever. We stood and gaped. Jason cried.

Jennifer ran toward Mom, begging her to stop. "Please, Mom, please stop. Please," she pled.

"You pick the Bible up off the ground, devil," the woman imitating our mom said. Then, she turned toward our sister. "Away," she said.

But Jennifer stood her ground, defying the woman.

"You're sick, Mom. Please."

"Can you see it? You see who he is? Look at him!"

Jason bent down and retrieved the Bible. His sobbing continued.

"Away!" she ordered.

We retreated into the living room, leaving Mom and Jason in the bedroom. A door slammed shut within the room. She had locked Jason in the closet, weeping. Then she left, locking the rest of us up in that big, two-story house, to get Dad's check. Jennifer waited a moment, then went into the bedroom to let Jason out.

But now that Mom had left, I figured, *Hey, things are looking better*. After all, going to get Dad's check on a Friday was doing something normal, performed like clockwork. She would be back at the house in no time with milk, bread, and, if we were lucky, rice with sugar and cinnamon sprinkled on top and baked with butter.

After a few hours, our mother had not come home. Well, maybe the checks weren't ready on time at Dad's work? It had happened before. A few more hours passed, and a bright, crisp December day gave way to a bruised purple sky.

Night fell, the lock turned. A woman hurried through the front door and then shut it as fast as possible. She twisted the lock and stood facing the door. She had long blonde hair and a flowing tan trench coat draped around her. As this strange woman slowly turned to face us children, she became recognizable. This peculiar grownup was our mother, wearing clothing and a coat she had not left the house in, not to mention a blonde wig.

Seeming to relax a little, she walked toward us and motioned for her children to gather around. We did as told. Squatting down, she quietly whispered to us she was being followed by evil people trying to kidnap not only her, but us as well, and that we should remain silent. She motioned for us to sit on the couch in the living room.

The quiet urgency of a parent, manic and imploring, telling you something serious is arresting. When a mom tells you bad people are after you and you need to be quiet, you're going to be as silent as possible. Most children would fidget and squirm. We didn't. I, for one, would've pissed my pants right there on that couch to avoid standing and casting a shadow on the floor. That could give away our location. No way in hell I'd walk to the bathroom or flush the toilet.

An hour later, our dad tried the door only to find it locked up tight. He knocked. Hard. Mom, seated at the kitchen table, turned her head with a vigorous snap toward us kids and her eyes pled with us to keep quiet. Sounding irritated, he belted out, "Open the door!"

Our older sister ran like a scalded dog to the door, despite our mom's protest. She unlocked the door, and he came inside.

"Why'd you lock the door?"

He turned toward the kitchen. He spotted our mother in a blonde wig and trench coat and with a pair of dark, round sunglasses covering most of the upper third of her face. Mom flew into her explanation about how sinister beings were coming to get her and if she didn't disguise herself, every one of us had no chance.

Dad, having been through several of Mom's "going" moments, asked her where she got the wig and clothing instead of addressing the bad people. She stated she bought it after picking up his check. This last bit of information was the proverbial straw that broke the camel's back.

"That money was for food, bills, and gas to get to and from work!" he yelled.

They argued back and forth for some time, Mom continuing to validate her reasons for what she had done and Dad asking where the remaining money was.

"How much do we have left?"

The answer came quickly. She told him every cent—all sixty goddamn dollars he had worked his ass off for—was being worn by our mother. Dad picked her up out of the chair she'd slumped in and began yelling loud enough to shake the peeling paint from the walls.

Mom got out of the hold Dad had on her and spun around and ran toward the kitchen counter. She opened the drawer, plucked out the biggest butcher knife we owned, spun around again and, at full speed, knife tightly gripped in her right hand, charged our father.

A man the size of our father makes for a big target, and it seemed for a moment that we were about to watch our mom kill our dad. But with relative ease, he side-stepped her, grabbed her by the wrist with one hand and popped her hand open, allowing the knife to skitter across the floor. The second that sharp bastard hit the floor, I was looking for somewhere to hide. Honestly? Seeing Mom going after Dad with a knife and hearing that shrill scream coming out of her got me thinking, *I may be next*.

It was at this point I found cover under that stained, shitty couch and cried. I covered my ears, closed my eyes, and whimpered as the screaming between my parents went on and on. My dad pled with my mom, telling her she needed help. My mom just... screamed. The hollering lightened up some after a while and, with a wet face and eyes locked shut, still covering my ears, I fell asleep.

The next thing I knew, I was being pulled out from underneath the couch and placed into the back of the police car. My two brothers, John and Jason, both older than me, joined me in the back seat. We pulled away from the Mansion for what would be the last time in our lives, unaware of what lay ahead. If we knew, we would have hidden. We would have prayed. We would have run like hell.

CHAPTER FOUR

As we pulled away from the curb, I could see our mother being loaded into the back of an ambulance on a gurney by two emergency techs. We rolled off into the dark night, not really saying anything. There was no plexiglass partition between us and the officer. He looked back at the three of us and, from to time, muttered things like "we're almost there" or "you boys okay?"

It only took fifteen or twenty minutes to pull up in front of a large, brick, three-story building surrounded by a ten-foot-tall, chain-link fence. The policeman came around, opened the door, and shuffled my brothers and me out of the back of the car. He led us up the steep stairs through the chilly night air, pulled the glass double doors open, and instructed, "Go on inside, boys."

Then he left us with the man in charge. After that, events took place rather quickly. The man, probably in his thirties, led us through corridors and up steep staircases, stopping once to issue each of us a blanket and pillow. We arrived at a gray, steel door.

"Okay, boys. Everything is going to be okay."

As he opened the door, I could see through the dim light. Steel cots aligned in rows appeared, occupied with young men sleeping. The man told us to be quiet and led each of us to a cot. He took my bedding first. Sheets whispered through warm air, followed by a Vietnam era army blanket. He smoothed my pillow with obvious experience. He motioned me forward with a flip of the wrist in an abracadabra motion, having completed his well-practiced show.

"Keep quiet, now. Lay on down and get some sleep."

I did as I was told. While he worked his magic on my brothers' sleeping arrangements, my eyes adjusted to the darkened room a bit more and I could make out approximately twenty young men who appeared to be older than the three of us. Not one of them seemed to be awake. The man finished with our cots, gazed down upon us, and put his index finger to his lips.

"Shush."

I lay there, scared and wondering what was going on and where the heck I was. I don't remember how fast I fell asleep, but it couldn't have been too awful long.

The next thing I knew, it was morning, and I was waking up to the sound of boys talking and laughing. I sat up and looked around, confused. My brothers were already awake and sitting side-by-side on John's bunk. I joined them. Nobody talked to us or even paid us much attention other than a quick glance. They went about their business, making the beds they'd slept in and pulling on t-shirts and Tough Skin jeans. Finally, a boy in his teens came over to the three of us and introduced himself.

"I'm Eddie," he said.

He eyeballed each of us, kind of sizing us up. He nodded his head at John and stated, almost with psychic foresight, "No matter where you guys go, no matter where you guys end up, *you* are the oldest brother, and *you* need to look after these two."

He hooked his thumb toward me and Jason. This young man, Eddie, had probably been in boys' homes or foster homes most of his life. Looking back at that moment, I realized two things: one, that young man must have been through some shit at an early age, and two, Eddie did not know, and could not have known, what lay ahead and the enormous responsibility and incredible burden that he had just laid at the feet of our oldest brother.

We three boys only spent a grand total of five days in that children's facility. While we were there, the staff treated us well and the young men we roomed with, mostly guided by Eddie, took to us like they were our protectors. They would enthusiastically take turns teaching us the proper way to make our cots and keep our area of responsibility tidy and clean.

Other boys would make sure we brushed our teeth and combed our hair after showers. They taught us how to manipulate the old milk dispenser in the cafeteria that had a large, steel arm jutting out the front of the monstrosity. With my glass in place under a cut tube, I'd pull downward on the big lever and ice-cold milk would flow in a steady stream into my cup. To this day, it was some of the coldest, most delicious milk I have ever tasted.

In the afternoons, the older boys had classes for arithmetic, writing, and reading. During these times, we sat at a picnic table, weather permitting, and were given board games and coloring books to entertain us. We had no idea at the time that our sisters were being cared for at the opposite end of the extensive building.

Jennifer, the oldest of us five kids, would ask her care providers if she could see John, Jason, and me. They told her that mingling between the boys and girls wasn't allowed. However, when we would sit and play at the picnic table, the staff allowed her to look at us from a large window on the third floor.

She later told us, "I waved my arms back and forth in the window, but you boys never seemed to look my direction."

As far as we knew, she and Julie, the youngest, were elsewhere or still at home. She would stay in the window and stand watch over us scribbling and playing until the people in charge of us would lead my brothers and me up the stairs to the entryway and out of sight. One day, she asked to go to the window and realized we were no longer there. Her next glimpse of us was approximately one year later.

After five days, it came time for my brothers and me to leave the boys' institution. A woman named Virginia, a dark-haired, portly state social worker, had been assigned to our case. She introduced herself that morning and informed the three of us we would not be going home but would stay with a nice family for a short period of time.

"Your mom is really sick, and we feel it's in your best interest to be kept a little longer until she's better," she said.

After gathering what little clothing we had, she directed us to the backseat of her car and away we went. Naturally, we asked several questions during the trip.

"How long until we get to go home?"

"Are Jennifer and Julie going to be with us?"

Virginia gave us no timeline on when we would return to our family. She told us that our sisters would not be joining us. We took a road trip that lasted about thirty minutes down the highway. Before long, we turned down a long, dirt and rock driveway that led to a medium-size, white farmhouse.

Trimmed in forest green, pastureland and scattered barns surrounded the home, with pens full of enormous pigs attached to the sides and backs of the large outposts.

As we pulled up to the gate to the farmhouse, I vividly remember what I saw to my left, out the back window: a large, white and gray speckled horse laying on its side, bloated and dead. A man was wrapping a log chain around the dead horse's upper body.

Virginia came to a stop, and we were let out of her car and greeted by the powerful aroma of hog shit. The man was hooking the chain to the back hitch of a green tractor. He stopped what he was doing and glanced our direction. He smiled and began walking toward us and, after looking us over, removed his gloves and shook Virginia's hand.

Virginia told us to stay by the car because she needed to speak with Mr. Sullivan. They left us by the car and walked toward the fence that surrounded the house and began chatting out of earshot. Meanwhile, we just stood, staring at the bloated, dead horse and taking in the naturally occurring fragrances of farm life.

After Virginia and Mr. Sullivan finished their conversation, they came back to where we waited. Virginia told us she would leave now, and Mr. and Mrs. Sullivan would settle us in. She told us she would check on us from time to time. She slid herself into her car, started it, and pulled away down the long drive.

"Well, boys, follow me."

His stained glove beckoned.

Instead of going into the warm house and out of the dropping temperature of nightfall, we followed Mr. Sullivan in a line over to the horse. He finished hooking the large link of the chain to the hitch of the tractor. He turned to us and gave us a 1970s circle of life explanation about how nothing went to waste. I learned that evening that, "Pigs got to eat, too!"

As he climbed up in the tractor's seat, he told us to follow behind the horse, but not too close. Again, in a line ranging from oldest to youngest, we did. He dragged the bloated horse two hundred yards through a large, galvanized gate and came to a stop. He dismounted, unhooked the chain from the tractor and from the horse, and turned to us and instructed us to head back the way we had come. When we got back through the gate, he pulled the tractor through and got off and shut and chained the opening. He walked us over to the fence by the house.

"Hang back."

Then he walked to each pig pen and turned them hogs loose into the pasture and I'll be damned if they didn't haul ass in a beeline straight to that dead horse!

He said, "Won't be much of her left when they get done with her."

Like I said, circle of life, pre-Lion King.

After the hogs received their meal, we then had ours. Mr. and Mrs. Sullivan were decent and kind people. They settled us in, made sure we had our baths and a warm room to share with plenty of blankets.

We still wanted to see our mom, dad, and sisters, but being treated kind by parental figures was better than the cold and gray boys' home.

It didn't take us long over the next few days to settle in and learn chores were part of country living and, to be honest, it wasn't bad. There was structure and always something to do or a moment to learn. We slopped hogs and cleaned stalls. We fed chickens and gathered eggs (my favorite chore). Much to my surprise, some eggs had a pink or green tint on the shells, and I thought that was really neat. The eggs tasted the same, but I guess I was half expecting mint or strawberry flavors to accompany them.

They enrolled us in the local school, and that was our lives for a couple of months. We occasionally asked when we could see our family or when we could go home. It was always the same answer: "Not yet."

We made friends and did well at school. Sometimes, Mrs. Sullivan would give us a little pocket change earned from chores that would allow us to purchase a jelly-filled donut and a carton of white milk from a squeaky cart the cafeteria lady would wheel to each classroom in the mornings.

Winter came, and the snowfall was deep. We each got warm clothing directly from the state, delivered to us by Virginia, who checked on us. On that visit, she informed us we would most likely be going home soon, which had us boys floating on cloud nine. After that, we counted the days and went about our schooling and chores with something to look forward to. I almost felt like we were leaving these kind people short-handed. I had become an integral part of the farm.

The day came when we arrived back to the farm on the school bus and made the long walk up the drive, which had been scraped fresh by the tractor and now had all the snow pushed to the edges. When we got to the house, Mrs. Sullivan informed us we'd be picked up that evening and heading home.

Overjoyed and grinning ear to ear, we dashed out to the front yard that faced the long drive and played.

We took empty feed tubs and filled them with snow, made brick-style snow forts and played capture-the-flag, all the while beaning each other with a good stockpile of snowballs. We would stop long enough to glance up the drive to the road access every time headlights appeared on the horizon.

"That looks like Dad's car!"

Nope, not that time. Again–

"That's Dad!"

Nope, not him.

This happened at least a dozen times before, finally, a familiar car was turning down the drive. It was a little red Datsun. Our dad didn't drive a little red Datsun. Virginia drove a little red Datsun.

Well, I assumed, *she's here to pick us up and take us home.*

The old phrase about asses and assuming applies here. The joy and anticipation we had been experiencing was immediately cut short and followed by tears when Virginia told us we would not be going home. Instead, we would go to our new, permanent foster home. We had just settled in and gotten used to being here and now away into the night we were to go again.

Virginia explained that Mr. and Mrs. Sullivan only took children in temporarily and that our time with them was up. A new family was willing to burden or task themselves with keeping three young brothers together instead of separating us.

The Sullivans helped us gather our things and put them in the car. We said our goodbyes and slowly drove down the long drive, looking out the back window as the farmhouse disappeared behind us. Longing for home and family, and again dreading starting over somewhere else, down the highway we went.

The overcast, gray sky faded to black as we turned left and headed westward. I didn't know at the time, but we were only eight miles from the doorstep of the Mansion. Later in life, when I joined the Army and was fortunate enough to be assigned to Fort Bragg, North Carolina, we would do physical training. Our battery commander loved to run. Occasionally, we'd do eight mile runs during the week and we'd complete this distance, along with stretches and cool downs, all before breakfast, almost like it was nothing.

Eight miles to our house from that corner, man. Eight fucking miles.

CHAPTER FIVE

Now a fully grown adult who can damn well drive himself, I find myself riding in the back of a police cruiser for the second time in my life. John can't boast the same low count. They have him cuffed and stuffed in the car in front of mine, leading the way to the police station and, of course, he's kicking at the partition as he had as a young adult. In his early days, this was standard operating procedure for him. Dad made several trips to the local police station when John returned from the Army, only to find that he'd went a couple of rounds with Johnny Law.

On one occasion, he had slipped his arms between his legs and chewed through the zip-ties that held him at bay. When the arresting officer had walked by the window of the room they were holding his drunk ass in, he kicked the glass out and the cop ended up in the emergency room, getting slivers of glass removed from his eyes.

He damn sure stepped up his game on this one.

"Is your brother that big of a fuckup?"

I look up to catch the officer's eyes, brows turned down and angry, smoldering in the rearview mirror.

"I don't know, officer," I reply. "Why don't you radio your buddy up ahead, ask him to pull over. You could take the cuffs off and ask him yourself."

His head remains still, but his slate-gray eyes and thick, salt-and-pepper mustache keeps darting back and forth from the road to the mirror.

"Well, douchebag, tonight he fucked up big time."

I continue looking ahead through the windshield. John seems to have quit kicking and is sitting there, barking something to the occupants in the front seat of his ride.

No talking your way out of this one, bro, I think. *No amount of hooting or hollering is stopping this train.*

"Did you get your kicks right along with him?" the officer growls, dried spit caking the corners of his mouth.

"I have the right to remain silent... anything I say can and will be—"

"Fuck you, prick!" he bellows, cutting my smartass rendition short.

"I don't know if you took part, but I can tell you one thing: your brother's gonna swing, dickhead, and you can take that to the bank!" His eyes are darting rapidly. "He murdered a good man, a great husband, and one hell of a father."

The last phrase brings a slight, auditory chuckle from behind my lips.

"That's right," he says. "Keep laughing, you little prick. I'll pull over right now and beat your goddamn head in."

You didn't know the fat bastard as much as you think you did.

"Make sure you clean the semen coating your lips under that pecker duster you call a mustache first, officer. You wouldn't wanna leave DNA behind, you delusional fuck."

When we arrive at the station house of what one might call "Podunk", John is already being pulled inside through a back door, fighting them the whole way. We come to a stop and Officer Crusty Lips opens my door, helps me out, and, with great accuracy, drives his right knee into my nuts, doubling me over.

"I hope them raisins swell up like basketballs and pop, you little prick."

He finishes with a heavy forearm between the shoulders.

Hello, asphalt.

I writhe around for a while, insides melting in an explosion of fiery agony. Once the pain recedes a bit, I look up and see him standing there, one hand on the butt of his service weapon, staring down at me.

"Any other comments from the fucking peanut gallery, boy?"

Not letting me answer, as if I could at the moment, he reaches down and jerks me to my unsteady feet and shoves me against the rear fender. I take this opportunity to brace my hips and recover. The cold sweat beading on my forehead feels good, considering the state of my balls and upper back. My wrists are aching from the steel rings holding them behind me. I figure this is the least of my worries now. He grips my right arm and squeezes, which will leave fingerprint bruises on my flesh.

"He was resisting," he conveys later.

I know his kind. You can always spot them. He's overweight or skinny as a rail in high school, picked on daily and doing nothing to stop it. After graduation, he seeks a career where he lies to himself and says it's making a difference, but then abuses the authority given to him. He seeks retribution against those that hurt his precious feelings not so long ago. Bribing speeders, feeling up female perps during the act of frisking. He never, and I mean never, gives anyone a break with a warning. That's his kind alright. He'll go home after his shift is over and brag to his ugly-ass wife about how much of a hero he was, and she'll believe him.

"The smartass, little prick mouthed me, and I had to straighten him out."

"I'll bet you did, baby."

"I'll tell you something else. He won't be dunking his donuts in his old lady for a while," he'll say, opening the paper.

"You sure put him in his place, baby."

She'll pour his coffee, serve him his greasy breakfast, and coddle him all morning until he's sawing logs and soiling the sheets with farts that smell like sulfuric eggs or turned fruit. She sneaks off to the bathroom where she'll twist the cap on her vibrator.

The way he abuses himself through food and drink, his life insurance and pension would come in handy.

She dreams.

CHAPTER SIX

W e'd been on the road for an hour and a half when we passed a
defunct church with a small, crooked steeple positioned on the
northeast corner of the country road we'd been traveling down. Even
though there were no interior lights in the old church and–of course,
being out in the country–no streetlights illuminating its snow-covered
grounds, I could make out the silhouettes of large and small headstones
behind the structure. The moonlight revealed old grave markers that
varied in height and width and spread across the backside of the place,
like sentries permanently standing guard on a cold winter's night. It
wasn't ominous, but just sort of... out of place atop the pastureland that
surrounded the church.

Virginia turned the little red Datsun south, slowly idling down the
snow-packed gravel road away from the church. A half mile down, to the
east, sat a ranch-style farmhouse, red brick halfway up from the ground
and finished with shiplap siding. We inched into the drive and came to a
rolling stop. A hedgerow ran to the right of the drive and a large backyard adorned with a winter-battered weeping willow stretched out to the
left.

Wood fencing cordoned off the backyard about thirty yards behind
the house, with a massive, red and white, weather-worn barn hulking
behind the fence row.

Several pieces of farm equipment lined the fence. I did not know the names or purpose of most of them. Two dogs trotted together from the barn toward the Datsun.

Virginia killed the engine and, like before, told us to exit the car. As we did, the two dogs, one yellow and one black and white, sidled up to us. The three of us boys started petting them. Their tails wagged, and they became more excited and began jumping up and placing their front paws on us. Covered with wet paw prints and a little dog slobber, we followed Virginia up the front walk toward the front door of the house.

We climbed the steps to the door, light flooding the porch as it opened. When our eyes adjusted, a woman was standing in the doorway. Her hair was salt and pepper and cut short to the nape. She wore glasses resembling those of Mrs. Beadles, the schoolteacher from *Little House on the Prairie*.

She opened the glass storm door that protected the interior entry and stepped to her left, motioning all of us inside.

"Well, who do we have here?" the woman asked. Her voice was pleasant and low, and she smiled at the three of us. Her teeth were yellowed and not in good shape.

"How are you, Carol?" Virginia asked.

The woman, Carol, replied she was fit as a fiddle. Virginia turned to us and again, just as she had done at Mr. and Mrs. Sullivan's house, told us to "stay still" right there because she needed to talk to Carol. Carol surveyed us one more time, the same smile having never left her mouth.

They walked through the living room and into the adjoining dining room with a really nice, family-size dining table and eight chairs centered just right. They disappeared through the opening and turned right.

Directly in front of us on the wall were the smiling faces of at least two-dozen children, each framed and obviously taken at school.

Soon we would learn they were kids this family had cared for over the years, children that had been removed from situations like the one we had been enduring or worse. I'm unsure of what events occurred that landed them in this home. Maybe they were better, maybe they were worse.

A man appeared from the dining room entryway. He was approximately six feet tall and went about one hundred and ninety pounds. The man wore glasses, only his were thicker and made his eyes appear larger.

He had graying hair over his lip. A twisted, waxed, handlebar mustache curled up at the ends.

"Hello, boys," he said. "My name is Arthur."

He never broke stride. He continued past us and hooked a left down a darkened hallway. After a few minutes, Virginia and Carol appeared from the dining room, Carol's lips now pursed.

"I'll be back to check on you boys soon," Virginia said. She thanked Carol and, just like that, was out the door, closing it behind her.

Carol told us to remove our shoes and coats and leave them right there in the doorway. We followed her through the kitchen, where we were told to enjoy cold milk accompanied by a small bowl of brown beans and a hunk of cornbread.

Having not eaten before leaving the other farm, we were hungry. It didn't take long to finish what she treated us to. Between bites, each of us told her a little about ourselves. She sat listening, only interrupting to inquire about our dad, mom, or sisters. I guess Virginia filled her in on our current situation.

As we finished our food, Carol left the kitchen. We placed our bowls and glasses in the kitchen sink and made our way back to the living room. John spotted the console television and twisted it on. We sat down on the floor as the old set warmed up. Pretty soon, Arthur returned to the living room and plopped down in a recliner, freshly showered and in pajamas, still not paying us much mind. Then a young man around John's age emerged from the darkened hallway.

"Hi, I'm Robbie," he said.

We said "Hi" in unison, telling him our names. Robbie let us know that Arthur and Carol were his mother and father and that he was their *actual* son, unlike the children on the wall. He started pointing at each picture and saying the name of the child in it. Some he didn't know because he hadn't been born yet. He droned on until Arthur told him that was enough and to "sit down". Robbie sat on the couch. He let out a sound through his clenched teeth. "Chuh." We later learned that when Robbie was disgusted or didn't get his way, he would make that noise. "Chuh, chuh, chuh."

Around the time Robbie was being shut down by Arthur, a voice came from behind us.

"It's bath time. I don't care which one goes first, but you boys decide and get it started."

We looked back at Carol and in her right hand she held a flyswatter. No sooner did we look at each other than Carol spoke again, louder, angrier, "I'm going to count to ten and one of you better decide!"

I looked back at Arthur and Robbie. Both were smirking.

Carol began counting,

"One... two... three... four! Five! Six! Seven, eight nine, ten!"

She began smacking us about as hard as you could with that damn thing. To begin with, we didn't know where the bathroom was in the house because we had yet to get the grand tour. And who the fuck counts that fast, like an auctioneer? All the while, Robbie was laughing his ass off and Arthur was encouraging her.

"Get them, Carol... Get them!"

Something is wrong.

That's all I could think while sitting in that tub, inspecting the red, waffle-like welts on my arms and shoulders. *Something is just not right with these people.*

Our first introduction to three of the eight members of the Ward family went just as quick as that. The brief introductions of Arthur, Carol, and Robbie, followed by the first salvo, the proverbial shot heard round the world—aka the flyswatter—was our welcome to our newest living arrangements and the type of bizarre and abusive behavior that would totally and completely envelop the three of us.

After we'd had our baths, Carol showed us through the kitchen, a typical one-counter, galley-style cooking area with a small, tin folding table and two chairs adorning the opposite wall.

If you advanced further, you arrived at a small alcove where the back door was located, leading to the previously described fenced-in backyard. A person either walked outside or, as we soon learned, took a right to a narrow staircase that led down to a dank, musty basement with a solid concrete floor and two low-watt bulbs that didn't provide adequate light for such a space.

In a corner in the basement on the back wall were two full-size beds with three pillows, yellowed from age, and one patchwork quilt per bed. On the same wall was a light-colored, non-descriptive pine door. It was not an exit. It was an entrance. And what lay and slept behind that door was a grown man. An adult, my brothers and I would soon enough learn.

His name was Walter, and he was the fourth of six children Arthur and Carol would bear. He wasn't short or tall, around five feet, ten inches tall. His weight went approximately two hundred and twenty pounds. He wasn't muscular or fit in appearance. The weight he carried, he did not carry well. He looked doughy and thick. His gut would spill over the waistband of his jeans, held up by a leather belt. The pearl-snap, button-up shirts he wore would strain to the point of opening without the aid of his sausage-like fingers.

Thinning, black hair rounded his pinched and pudgy face out. He had a thick, black mustache drooping past the corners of his mouth. His eyes were situated close together and half-obscured by thick, tinted, prescription glasses. Walter was one of those kids in his youth that sat at the dining-room table, begging his mother, "Please Momma, please. Just one more spoonful of gravy."

From the looks of it, Momma always caved and ladled it on thick, high, and deep.

After being directed to the basement, the three of us fell to sleep rather quickly.

Our awakening the next morning would seem much longer and would set the tone for the next thirteen months.

An unexpected eruption awoke us the next morning. Walter pulled our blankets off of us and began yelling that lazy pigs were not to be tolerated and we had better get used to pulling our weight. After lining us up next to the beds, he inspected them. He was looking for piss stains, something we would learn he very much hated.

"Bingo, we have a winner," he said.

John won the grand prize that day. Walter pulled his leather belt from his overflowing waist with relative ease and then shoved John to the ground. We'd never been put through what took place next—ever. Sure, our dad had spanked us with his hand across the ass when needed, and we learned valuable lessons when it happened. But this was different.

Walter tore into John, beginning at the top of his back and slashing at the back of his knees. Jason and I stood watching in disbelief and horror at the violence we were witnessing. Each loud crack of leather on

John's skin was followed by a kind of screaming I'd never heard come from my oldest brother.

After every lash from the leather belt, a new, bright-pink stripe appeared across the backside of John's body like a disjointed angry game of tic-tac-toe.

"Sinner! You goddamn sinner!" Walter bellowed.

John tried to crawl across the basement floor to escape the belt. Walter reached down and dragged him back within striking distance. Then the whole ordeal reset, with John crying out in pain and Walter letting John know how much he had let God down with every swing of the belt.

"You goddamn sinner! You goddamn good for nothing sinner!" His words echoed off the concrete walls.

The beating ended after it seemed John could take no more. He hoisted himself up on all fours, tears steadily streaming down his face and whimpering like a beat dog and grasping his lower back. The welts were slowly turning an enraged purple right before our eyes.

It was about that time round two started.

Walter pulled his right leg back and swiftly swung it forward, aimed directly at John's ass. The cowboy boot on Walter's foot connected squarely with John's backside and sent him flying forward and back to the surface of the dirty cement floor. At that moment, John began gasping for air and curled up in the fetal position, trying desperately to catch his breath. Another kick to his lower back stretched him out and he began contracting and extending his body like a slug after being doused with salt.

"Get on your damn feet!" Walter roared.

After catching his breath, the actual work for John began. He pulled himself to his feet, chest hitching and still struggling for air.

"Strip that sheet from the bed and throw it in the washing machine," Walter barked.

John removed the sheet from the bed, whimpering the whole time.

"Now, buddy boy, grab that mattress and haul it up the stairs," he said.

John pulled the piss-soaked mattress by the handles the factory had sewn to the sides. It hit the floor with a thump and John began sliding it across the floor. Walter hauled off and kicked him in the rear again. John hit the floor. Another kick in the ass, and another, which sent tears rolling down John's face again.

"Stand the mattress up on its side, stupid," Walter yelled.

John flinched, half-expecting another kick to the posterior. Walter allowed him to get back to his feet and stand the stained mattress on its side.

"Get it upstairs, you pissing little sinner," he reminded him.

Walter turned to Jason and me.

"You two don't move a goddamn muscle or you'll join that little bastard."

We stood statue-still and didn't move or say a word. I don't remember breathing much either. By this time, John had made it to the base of the stairs and was struggling to manipulate the heavy load up them. Walter caught up to him with another kick, only this time John did not fall or lose his balance or cry out. He just continued dragging that heavy bastard up the wooden basement stairs. When he reached the top, he came face-to-face with the back door.

"I'll get the door for you, you little baby," Walter said. "Only little babies piss the bed."

He opened the door and John continued outside. After several minutes and muffled shouts from Walter, John made his way back down the stairs, with Walter closely following. He made Jason and me sit on the bed we had shared the night before and had John stand so he wouldn't get any pee from his underwear on the clean bed. John had stopped crying and Walter stood before us, glaring back and forth between us.

"You three will *not* come into *my* house and piss in the beds we provide to you. If you want to act like animals, then you will be treated like animals."

It terrified us, having never had an experience that compared to this event. Then he said something I'll never forget, all the while smirking as though he'd just kicked the shit out of the toughest man on the planet.

"As long as you're here, you three are mine. If you think they care upstairs what the hell happens down here, think again. Piss the bed or don't do as you're told and I'll beat the three of you within an inch of your lives."

He then walked toward his bedroom door and turned around and told John to go clean up and then mumbled "bastards" as his door closed behind him.

Back home, John was more or less known as a pretty tough kid on our block and at school, having won several school-yard fights and arguments. He was never arrogant about it and rarely picked fights with other kids, though he finished them. When John looked up at Jason and me, he wasn't the same confident, brave older brother we were used to being around. Our brother was scared and humiliated. Beaten down and defeated, he was no longer himself and, after that morning and the ass kicking he took, he would never be the same.

CHAPTER SEVEN

Almost as quick as Walter disappeared back into his basement bedroom, Arthur entered and stood halfway down the basement stairs.

"I see the three little pigs have met my son Walter," he said.

He traversed the last few remaining stairs. John was stifling his tears as best he could. Arthur reached into the dark cubby underneath the stairs and retrieved an old boot, worn out from God knows how many years of working their farmland or administering one too many ass kickings to the children in the pictures hung on the wall upstairs. Then, with great accuracy, he fired the boot at John. It glanced off his shoulder, struck Jason right square in the ear, and fell to the floor. Tears filled Jason's eyes and slight sobbing started up.

"Don't you start up, too!" Arthur ordered.

I stood as motionless as before and averted my eyes away from my brothers and our new foster father. Jason quickly brought his audible cries under control.

"My son told you to get your ass upstairs and clean yourself up, you little pissant," Arthur growled.

John, still sniffling, shuffled past him and headed up the stairs and out of sight. It wasn't hard to figure out that Arthur had listened in and, for all we knew, observed his son beating the hell out of our older brother. He had stood by and let it happen! The bastard just let his son kick the shit out of John and never intervened or uttered a single word to stop him.

"You two get dressed," he said. "Chores need doing."

With that, he clomped back upstairs, the sounds of his boots fading toward the opposite end of the house.

"I'm scared," I announced to Jason.

"Shush!" He pointed at Walter's door. "You want him to come back out here, Dipshit?"

John returned to the basement and joined us without a word. We made our way upstairs to the gallery, where we were greeted by the smell of frying bacon and the sight of Carol manning the skillet on the stove-top, alongside a small pot emitting steam from its opening. Arthur made his way into the kitchen and instructed us to follow him outside. Carol had hung our coats on hooks by the back door. We put them on and made our way down the back steps.

"Get on the pickup," he said.

We started toward the passenger door to get in the front.

"Not in the truck," he said. Pointing to the flatbed attached to the back of the cab, he instructed, "Crawl on up."

Doing as we were told, we clambered up. Then we heard Arthur say, "Hold on."

Hold on? To what? There were no rails and no tailgate. He started the old truck up.

We kept as tight a grip as we could on the sides of the flatbed as he drove toward the barn. The bumpy terrain dislodged our hold multiple times, and we scrambled to keep our balance as he sped up and slowed down in jerks. Once we arrived, he didn't wait for us to recover, but started barking orders on how to stack hay.

Already huffing and puffing in the chilly morning air, we loaded square bundles of gold grass onto the back of the truck. My brothers and I struggled to load the heavy bales which, I'd find out later, usually averaged fifty to seventy pounds. It wasn't a simple task for three skinny kids who'd never done this type of chore before.

"Looks like you boys need to put on a little more ass," Arthur said.

He was kind of laughing when he suggested this. His chuckling lightened the mood and eased a little of the fear that had lingered from what had taken place earlier... Could it have been an isolated incident? With luck, if we minded our behavior and actions, we would be fine and that'd be the last time they would administer a whooping like that.

After working up a good sweat, we climbed aboard the S.S. Hay Hauler and grabbed hold of the baling wire that encompassed each side of the bales from top to bottom. Arthur cranked the lorry over and we were off, headed east over uneven pastureland. The sun was casting a dark hue in the sky and on the land. Dawn was upon us and provided just enough light to make out slow-moving, lumbering shapes making their way to the truck. After a quarter mile or so, Arthur came to a stop and got out of the rig, holding two plier-style tin snips in his hands. He handed one to Jason. Arthur then gave us a quick tutorial on baling-wire snipping. He took a wire between the pliers and, under some tension, the wire popped and sprung up like a jack-in-the-box.

"That's why you keep your head pulled back and away from the bale. That wire will take an eye or cause quite a cut," he said.

He handed John the other pair of snips and asked, "Did you see what I did?"

John said he had and reached down, leaned back, and snipped a wire. It popped much like Arthur's example had and the bale spread apart. Arthur told me to pull both pieces of strand from under the bales and lay them up by the front of the truck cab at the back of the flatbed. I did as I was told, happy to be included and part of the process we had just learned.

"Now kick that hay down to the ground and then move back to the next bale and do the same thing until they're all cut and kicked."

John and Jason booted the loose hay from the back end of the truck and then moved to the next bale. After we got into a rhythm of sorts, we dispatched wires and hay began flying pretty quick to the ground. It was almost like a game. All the while, the cows that had intercepted the truck ignored us and dug into the hay.

When the task was complete, Arthur climbed behind the wheel and we loaded into the back of the truck and headed toward the barn up by the house. As we got closer, I could make out a dingy, rectangular object resting upright against the backside of the house. It was John's piss-stained mattress. The feeling of self-worth and the good vibe I'd been experiencing from learning something new drained out of me, replaced with a tinge of fear.

The sight of it brought back that morning's ass kicking John had taken. I realized I was shaking. Was it the cold temperatures that December morning? Or was it the fact Arthur's son, Walter, had brutalized John?

We unloaded from the truck and followed Arthur into the barn. Walter was there, but was exiting out of the structure through a side door without a glance.

"Have one of you ever milked a cow?" Arthur asked.

We hadn't. He went about grabbing a small wooden stool and a galvanized bucket.

He said, addressing a large, fat, tan, milk cow, "Good girl, good girl, Yeller."

He positioned himself toward her back end and put the stool down by the bulging sack that hung below her. She bellowed a bit. I learned that if you didn't milk her regularly, it could be painful for her. Arthur reached under Yeller and grasped a teat and pulled downward and, low and behold, milk squirted right out and pinged the bottom of the bucket.

He reached with his other hand and began double fisting that udder like there was no tomorrow. The bucket was two-thirds full when he finished and handed it to Jason and told him to take care and not spill any milk. He cut Yeller loose into the pasture and we followed him back up to the house, mattress growing larger.

"Go on inside and give that bucket to Carol," he told Jason.

Jason went in and Arthur turned to me and John.

"You don't wet the bed like this pissant, do you?" he said, looking at John with disgust.

John's head had just raised back up after the morning's chores and, just like that, his eyes were back down at his feet, ashamed.

"I don't think so," I said.

"You better know so, young man, or you'll get what he got this morning. Now, you boys go inside."

We opened the door and the aroma of bacon hit us smack-dab in the face. Carol was straining the milk through cheesecloth into a metal pitcher. Jason sat at the small table in the even narrower kitchen. An extra folding chair added to the end made three, so John and I took our places with Jason.

Fried eggs, bacon, and toast sat on the kitchen counter, heaped on serving platters. The smell was maddening to me. I was hungry and couldn't wait to dig in. Carol took the platters, two on one arm and one in the other hand, and walked to the dining room, placing them in the center of the table that had four place settings. Robbie was at the dining-room table, where we would soon join him for this wonderful country breakfast.

Or that was what I had assumed.

When Carol returned, she dug three bowls out of a cabinet and put them in front of us. She turned and removed the small pot that had been steaming on the stove and began ladling malt-o-meal into each of our bowls.

She filled three cups with the milk Arthur had just extracted from Yeller and doled them out to us, along with three spoons.

"Eat up, boys," she said.

Meanwhile, Arthur had washed up and seated himself at the dining-room table with Walter and Carol. They held hands, bowed their heads, and Walter led the prayer, taking care to ask for the Lord's ever-loving family protection from the wickedness of the world and to guide the lowly people, that they may find the light and find salvation.

Amen.

They dug in and pretty well devoured the morning meal with little talk amongst them. Meanwhile, the tops of our meager breakfasts had formed a skin-like membrane over the mushy substance.

Carol hollered, "I said dig in, boys! Don't waste any of that food! We don't waste food in this house, savvy?"

We took up eating our fast-congealing malt-o-meal and finished it all along with the unpasteurized cups of milk. They then directed us to go to the bathroom, wet our hair, and wash up for church. At first, I thought nothing of it. Then, I realized it was Saturday. Since when did anybody go to church on Saturday?

The church, Seventh Day Adventist, observed what they called the Sabbath. Now, religion is religion all over the world. I was no expert on the practice of prayer or where, why, and how people choose to observe or practice their faith.

It was just odd to me because we had always gone to church with our mother on Sunday mornings or evenings and–sometimes–we attended Wednesday night services, so it was just different. Two things I will say about the place: one, someone actually featured us as singers on a weekly basis after the sermon, and that was kind of neat.

Two, we used to have to wash the feet of the higher-up, older men in charge and that was *not* kind of neat. It was gross. I later understood why we did it, but it was still an odious task.

After getting cleaned up, we loaded into the family car–a station wagon–and we left the farm, headed to town to be introduced to our new place of worship and its meager amount of members.

The small, white church rested a few blocks off the main highway that ran through the small town of Ridgeway, Kansas. When we entered the building, it was dark and there couldn't have been over twenty-five people attending, ninety-five percent of whom had to have been eligible for social security.

We ambled down the aisle, and Arthur motioned for us to take our seats. Looking around as I slid between the first two well-worn pews, I observed that almost everybody there was staring at us three boys. I'm sure they were used to seeing new kids from time to time in the company of the Wards, but they were curious about us. It could be that we were the only attendees, not counting Robbie, on the back end of life.

Regardless, they were gawking on with admiration for the Wards, what with them taking in these destitute boys who, without their good graces, would sin to no end.

A young man in his mid-twenties came over to our foster parents and leaned down, giving Carol a big hug. This man was another son, the third. His name was Frank Ward. He was much thinner than Walter, but he wore the same tinted prescription eyeglasses as Walter and the rest of the family. My guess is they received a buy-one-get-a-dozen-free or a family discount on their spectacles.

He gave us boys a small, polite wave and a bit of a smile and seated himself in the front row at the foot of the stairs leading up to the pulpit. After a few minutes, an attractive, red-headed woman with a child perhaps two years younger than me in tow sat next to Frank. The little boy, Thomas, seemed comfortable around Frank, not apprehensive or nervous. That was a good indicator that this man was nothing like his younger brother, Walter, or his parents. One could hope so, anyway.

Walter was not in attendance for the services that day, or any other. The way he lit into John that morning, I couldn't think of anybody who should pray for forgiveness more than him. His mother and father hadn't burst into flames yet, so he wouldn't either.

Although, thinking back on it now,if he had showed up and combusted in spontaneity, it would have not only warmed the cold air that permeated the old church, but if the congregation was quick enough and prepared for an old-fashioned picnic, we could have roasted hotdogs and marshmallows over his fat ass.

The sermon began. A ways into the preacher's teachings for the day, Frank whispered to his gal and got up and exited through a door at the back of the room.

He emerged about ten minutes later, holding an acoustic guitar, and stood patiently and quiet off to the side of the stairs that led up to the preacher. Now I was curious. We'd grown up around music, with our mother being one of the millions of Elvis Presley fans around the world and our dad listening to his outlaw country music. The likes of Merle Haggard, Johnny Cash, Waylon Jennings and, his favorite, the Possum, old George Jones, graced his eight-track collection.

The padre said, "Okay. Now, Frank Ward will perform a song for us this morning."

Frank proceeded up the stairs with his guitar slung across his button-up, starched, white dress shirt and a sheet of paper with lyrics scrawled on it clutched in his right hand. Arthur and Carol looked on with great anticipation, beaming with pride at their son. Frank took the sheet of paper, placed it on the pulpit, and stepped back. He strummed a few chords and seemed satisfied with the sound it emitted. Then, beginning with a G note, his performance began.

On a hill far away stood an old rugged cross,
The emblem of suffering and shame;
And I love that old cross where the dearest and best
For a world of lost sinners was slain.
So I'll cherish the old rugged cross,
Till my trophies at last I lay down;

I will cling to the old rugged cross,
And exchange it someday for a crown.

As Frank took the swing and headed into the second verse of the time-honored hymn, I began checking my ears for bleeding. I gave him props for effort, but man, that guy couldn't carry a tune in a bucket. The first sentence of the first verse was borderline baritone and the second sentence was damn near falsetto. His guitar skills were excellent, but holy smoke, that voice. Never had I ever heard a voice so out of tune and unable to decide what range the song should be in.

Jason began giggling, and I followed suit. Carol glared at the two of us.

Oh man, we're going to get it, I thought.

Over time, we would make up for it in spades. She would make sure of that.

CHAPTER EIGHT

After Frank completed his butchering of "The Old Rugged Cross", they afforded the three of us a custom in this church I'd never heard of in my life. We were told that they had selected us as the fortunate young fellas that would wash the feet of the Deacons. Less than twenty-four hours with this family and already receiving honors and coveted opportunities! Woo-hoo!

There were three folding, metal chairs at the base of the stairs and a trio of super old gentlemen, looking like mummies right down to their dusty, old wrappings that once were suits, took up position on each. In unison, they began pulling the legs of their pants up to their knees. Two of the men held the crumpled pant legs in their fingers, but the other guy was a different story. He produced two blousing rubbers from his pocket and cuffed his pants just below the knees. Well, this guy knew what he was doing, a real professional, and tenured no doubt.

The preacher had us kneel at their feet and remove their shoes, taking care to untie them and not slip or pry them off, definitely different from anything we had seen or taken part in at our church back home. Arthur appeared next to me, holding a tan, ceramic-type of mixing bowl adorned with dark brown crosses surrounding the entire rim.

"Take this and place it to the right of Mr. William's feet."

He placed the bowl in my hands and, as I brought it down to eye level, a white washcloth appeared in the water, completely submerged. I put the bowl to the right of the old man's feet and waited. The preacher said a few lines and then motioned to Arthur.

"Okay, Joseph, remove Mr. William's sock on your right, and then on your left, and place them across his shoes."

I looked up. Mr. William was looking down at me, smiling, with a look on his face that said, *Boy, are you in for one hell of a treat, son. You just picked all five white balls* and *the power ball.*

I looked back down at his socks and, just my luck, there was pet hair—not covering them, though. There was a good layer close to the soles, like he'd shuffled around the old linoleum floor in his kitchen, getting that morning's cup of coffee and, perhaps, dry toast.

The faint medicinal smell of some sort of topical cream, aerosol, or powder wafted, gentle yet invasive, up my nostrils. I thought, *That can't be good.* I'd seen commercials where some poor soul's feet were battling a fully involved hellfire and the only remedy was a wet spray, an application of some soothing cream, or a good dusting of itch relief talcum to douse them God-awful flames.

I hooked my index finger inside the top of Mr. William's left sock and pulled it downward. The plain black dress sock slid down his lower leg and revealed a freckled, hairless ankle canvassed with blue and purple, web-like, broken blood vessels. A spiraling roadmap to an end. I manipulated the sock over his heel, arch, and his toes.

His toes!

The first four toenails looked like gnarled, gold nuggets embedded in flaky, white, crusty canoes. Ah, but the pinky toe—the pinky toe was missing its nail, it was missing its tip... it was missing. Well, that was just great. I guess his little piggy went 'wee-wee' all the way home! The smell of whatever the hell he had used on his feet intensified. Thank God he'd opted to use something. I fear the natural smell of his feet might have had me vomiting or, at the very least, gagging on my malt-o-meal and milk.

"It ain't gonna bite ya, young feller," Mr. William said.

Okay, so he must have seen the look on my face. My eyes had to be bugging out of my head about right then. I deposited his sock on top of his shoes and then repeated the process as fast as I could on his right foot. All five toes were present and accounted for, but his right foot seemed flakier and his nails a bit more twisted. The sock snagged on his big toe because the nail curved to the left at a forty-five-degree angle. I unhooked it and placed it on top of the other sock, still not believing this was happening.

Arthur said, "Wring that cloth out and wash both of Mr. William's feet from heel to toes."

I reached in the tepid water and pulled the washcloth out and wrung it until it was damp.

"Good," Arthur said.

I went to work rubbing his left foot, heel to toe, as quickly as I could. I repeated the process on the right, then let the washcloth sink to the bottom of the water-filled bowl.

Arthur reached down and handed me a clean, white hand towel and instructed me to dry Mr. William's feet, so I did, left to right. After Mr. William's abominable feet were spic and span, Arthur's instructions were simple for the grand finale.

"Hand your brother the bowl and then have a seat back on the pew."

I handed the bowl to my left where Jason was kneeling, his blue eyes wide and begging me to delay the handing-off of the precious artifact, knowing what was coming. I laughed a little like I had when Frank was attempting to praise our Lord through what he interpreted as a song. Then Jason's expression changed.

Uh-oh. I'd seen that look before. Jason's eyes narrowed, and I knew he was going to let me have it for laughing at him once this was over and, as soon as he had the privacy he needed, he would kick my ass right proper. I couldn't help it, though. Why should I have all the fun? Brothers share, right?

I made my way back to my seat on the long wooden bench. With their backs to me, John and Jason hustled through the process with great speed. They had watched me, so they had a blueprint they could go by and the two of them made quick work of it and, one by one, found their seats next to me. Jason, still pissed I had laughed at him, was jabbing my ribcage when John finished and took his seat.

We didn't have to place the socks and shoes back on the Deacons' feet. That was a task they completed themselves, *Thank you very much.*

After they vacated the chairs they had been sitting in and returned to their seats, the preacher rattled off a few more quotes and then the services were over—but not for the three of us. Hymn books needed to be put up in the back room and the bowl, now containing the water and washcloth used to cleanse the feet of the higher-ups, needed taken back there as well. They had also designated this our tasks, or so Carol informed us as the congregation began saying their goodbyes to one another and talking about weekend plans and who was coming to visit.

"They did a fabulous job for their first time," I heard some older woman behind us say. She had studied, critiqued, and graded our every move.

"Darn near flawless," Arthur said.

As the parishioners cleared out, Carol said, "Joseph, pick up that bowl. John and Jason, gather all the hymn books and bring them to the back room through that door." She pointed to the door Frank had come out of earlier with his guitar.

So, as my brothers went around collecting the song books, I bent over and picked up the bowl, careful not to slosh it around.

"Don't spill it, kiddo," she said.

John and Jason soon joined us and we filed into the little room, with Carol leading the way. My brothers started looking for shelves to place the books on and I just stood there while she quietly shut the door. Pointing again, she said, "Just put them hymn books on that blue shelf."

The two of them started lining the books up on the shelf and I asked, "Where do I put the bowl of water?"

She nodded toward a small bathroom further back in the room. I headed that way, but after a couple of steps, Carol said, "Wait, kiddo. Your brothers need to finish first."

It certainly would not take the three of us to dump the bowl of water down the sink or commode, but alright, I'd wait. My brothers came back to where she and I stood. I looked up at her. She pursed her lips, eyes wide, cementing me in place.

"What was so funny out there today?" she hissed.

"The look on Jason's face when I was handing him the bowl," I said. When she said nothing, I went on, slightly stammering, "It was funny because he looked scared and then his face changed when I laughed at him."

I didn't know how else to explain why I laughed during the foot-washing ritual. I sure as hell didn't mean to disrespect their religious customs. Lines formed around her mouth as it turned downward into a frown.

"You know darn well know what I'm talking about," she said.

I told her I didn't, and I was sorry for laughing in church.

"My son," she hissed. "Three little heathens like you had the gall to laugh at my son during his performance."

"We're sorry," Jason voiced.

We looked back and forth at each other. Then a small, nasty smile spread across her face.

"Drink," she said.

Complete silence. A few muffled voices came from the other side of the door.

"What?" John said.

"I said drink. No sips. You drink right now."

In utter horror, I realized she meant to have us recycle this disgusting, hand-me-down water that was used to cleanse the elders' feet. John spoke up sharp and fast.

"No. You can't make us do that. It's not right."

"You shut your heathen mouth before you get what you got this morning," she said to him. "I'm going to count to ten and one of you had better drink."

Jesus Christ, she's counting again.

"Joseph, don't," John said.

She began, "One... two..."

"Joseph, don't!" he said louder.

"Three..."

"Joseph?"

"Four... five... six... seven, eight, nine, ten!"

The bowl flew from my hands and shattered into several large chunks on the floor. Water splashed around our shoes and spread across the floor.

John had jumped over and knocked the bowl clean out of my grasp and positioned himself between her, me, and Jason.

That's our brother, I thought. This was the old John that I knew from back home.

Carol's face contorted. Her lips curled, revealing yellow tombstone tusks.

"You're in big trouble, buddy," she snarled, looking straight at John.

"You can't treat us like this," he said. "I'm telling Virginia."

Just then, the door opened and Arthur poked his head in and looked around at us, then down at the broken ceramic bowl.

"What's going on in here?" he asked Carol.

Her eyes never left John, even when responding to her husband. "We'll talk about it at home... with Walter," she murmured.

Now she had the same look on her face she'd exhibited when Frank was singing earlier. She was beaming with pride at the thought of her fourth child straightening this little heathen out for daring to defy her, right here in the house of the Lord.

I'd never been prouder of my older brother up to that point in my young life. He had done as instructed by the older boy, Eddie, from the boys' home.

No matter what, protect your brothers. You're the oldest. It's your job.

Knowing what lay ahead of him after this act of defiance, they should have pinned a medal on him for his bravery.

"Clean this mess up with a towel, dump the leavings in the sink, and come back out front."

She exited stage left, leaving the door ajar.

"Hurry, boys," Arthur said, ducking out as well.

I picked up the broken pieces of the ceramic bowl and Jason grabbed the washcloth and ran into the bathroom and came back with a dry, white hand towel and began mopping up the water. John stood guard, staring at the door as I placed the shattered remains of the foot bowl in the trash. Jason and I washed our hands in the bathroom and then the three of us exited the back room, triumphant and, once again, heads held high, with John leading the way.

CHAPTER NINE

The car ride home was quiet and uneventful. The three of us boys already knew, having learned enough in less than twenty-four hours, it would bode well to keep our mouths shut and to stay out of the line of fire. Carol just sat there on the passenger side of the old station wagon, stewing in her own juices and God knows what thoughts. Arthur attempted small talk a couple times with her but was unsuccessful in eliciting any response from his wife. After two failed tries, I'm sure he realized that one, if not all three of us, had pissed her off.

When we arrived back at the farm, we all piled out of the car and made our way to the back porch.

"Stay outside, boys," Arthur said.

John was naturally thankful that he wasn't told to head to the basement and hook up with Walter. However, the fear of not knowing what plans lay ahead soon for John, or maybe even all three of us, was daunting. We walked over to the north side of the backyard, where a fence ran the length of the road all the way to the intersection by the old church. Four horses were grazing on grass that had poked through the thin clumps of snow that remained on the ground, most of which had melted away. One horse, Lightning, was a palomino. To this day, his name is the only one I remember of the four.

As we trudged up to them, they looked up, one by one, and I guess kind of sized us up. We held out our empty hands, not having anything to offer them. They sniffed our upturned palms a moment and went back to grazing.

We went about walking the fence line. Occasionally, a horse trailed alongside of us and we stopped to either reach through the fence to pet its bulging ribcage or to see if we could get its nose to our hands. After a while, the horses trailed off into the pasture and we took to exploring the perimeter of the backyard.

After about an hour, the dogs showed, and we showered them with attention and they gave it back as good as we gave it to them. We made our way over to the side of the barn and messed around for a bit. We came across a pile of dead branches and decided now was as good a time as any to have an old-fashioned sword fight.

"On guard, sir," Jason said.

We began parrying back and forth. Every time two of us made solid contact, the branch would break in half or simply crumble, only to be replaced by the next best stick of wood. This went on for some time, then—

"Hey, boys! Come on in and wash up! It's time to eat!"

We argued about who won which fight and who was the worst swordsman as we made our way back to the house. Why couldn't they just let us keep playing? I wasn't even hungry, and being inside usually spelled trouble.

When we entered through the kitchen, I noticed our table was no longer in its previous location. What they'd done was butt it up against the far end of the dining-room table.

"Come sit down," Walter said, pointing at the small table, accompanied by our folding chairs.

As we took our places, I noticed a man and woman we'd not yet had the privilege of meeting.

"This is Ken and this," Carol said, her hand sweeping through the air, "is Brenda, my daughter."

Brenda nodded her head. Ken didn't even acknowledge us. I'd say old Ken was more interested in what was on the table and not beside it.

"Hey, Dad, do you think these boys could help us clear some rocks from the back?" Brenda asked.

"Don't see why not. It ain't gonna hurt 'em none," Arthur replied.

"Okay, we'll get on that soon."

The dining-room table was brimming with food and it looked delicious. There were two baked chickens, perfect, golden, and glistening in their own juices. Vegetables, no doubt canned by this hornet's nest of a family, created a garden of Eden in each bowl. Butter melted down through the piles of green beans, peas, and carrots. They had loaded a plate with fluffy homemade bread and oily amber butter. There was a giant bowl of pillowy, white mashed potatoes and a large gravy boat filled with chocolate-brown gravy, still steaming from being added to the table at the very last second. Salt, pepper, and butter pooled atop a small pot of white navy beans.

We would come to learn that someone specifically prepared the navy beans for Walter, and only Walter, every Saturday. Nobody but him touched them.

Not really being that hungry when we'd been told it was time to eat had suddenly changed. These folks put on one hell of a spread. I couldn't wait to taste that rich, dark gravy on the clouds of white taters!

Arthur called for us to bow our heads and pray.

"Dear Lord, we thank you for the blessings you've given us and the trials we have endured. We thank you for this food that will nourish our bodies and bring us health and opportunity. Lord, we also want to thank you for guiding these three brothers to our door so that we may teach them your lessons and, with your help, we might help save them and steer them clear of the wicked path that their mother and father led them down at such a young age."

Wicked path? What the fuck?

He droned on and asked for his wife and children to be watched over, including their health and *blah, blah, blah.*

"In your name we pray, amen."

Besides the mild sting from verbally slamming us and our parents, it was the standard prayer you'd hear around most folks' tables on Sunday after church—except this was Saturday. I put it out of my mind and turned eagerly toward the food.

Over the lips and past the gums, look out stomach, here it comes.

The family began dishing up and remarking on how well Brenda did preparing the feast while they were at church. They were now spooning, ladling, drizzling, and dismembering their chickens lickety-split.

There was just one tiny, yet major, oversight taking place.

Every time a platter, bowl, or dish made its way to our folding table, it would make a hard turn to the right and head down the other side of the larger dining-room table. Meanwhile, Brenda got up and headed to the kitchen and, in mere moments, returned with a dish of cornbread and a saucepot filled with brown kidney beans.

"Get 'em while they're hot, fellas," she said.

That's when I noticed, for the first of many times, that when we sat down, we had bowls and spoons in front of us. And them? They had plates and a full set of flatware. What was this? Punishment for how we had giggled at Frank's terrible singing? Or for laughing during our little crash course in proper foot care? Maybe we were being disciplined for disobeying Carol's direct orders and not partaking in foot-water shots or for breaking the cross-covered bowl.

It had nothing to do with those things, though. This is what we ate that Saturday and every Saturday we were wards of the state and in the primary care of the Wards. Most of the time, we'd end up with some left-over green beans or peas, so we got our roughage, so to speak, but we never fully partook in the Sabbath meals they prepared.

After watching the family members attending dinner that day, devouring most of what was being served, we were lucky enough to each get some meat stripped from what they left on the chicken carcasses and a smattering of the mashed potatoes. They had inhaled the gravy. I didn't get to try that dark brown liquid I'd been coveting since I first caught sight of it.

Meanwhile, we finished our beans and cornbread and then were excused from our own little table. We didn't help clear the leavings or do dishes, except for taking our bowls and spoons to the kitchen sink.

"We wouldn't want one of you to drop the good china," Carol stated.

Instead, we were told to go back outside and play. That was just fine with me. The more distance we kept between us and them, the better our odds that we wouldn't have a run-in with one of them.

So back outside we went, wandering around the perimeter of the yard, seeking ways to entertain ourselves. After some time had passed, John said, "Well, looks like I'm not in trouble for breaking the bowl."

Perhaps he was right. Maybe after a good meal and time to cool down, bygones were bygones and they could chalk up the church standoff between Carol and him as a push.

Arthur called us inside, directing us to the living room. Carol was just seating herself at an electric organ and studying sheet music. We took a seat on the floor, facing her, and she played. Some songs we had heard while attending our old church back home and some we'd never heard before—at least, as I recall. This was a Sabbath tradition the family adhered to religiously—no pun intended—every Saturday evening. When she'd finished up, dusk was just peeking through the large picture window that faced west from their living room.

"Bath time," she exclaimed.

All three of us were on our feet and tripping over each other to get to the tub first. Call it "flyswatter" conditioning. In no particular order, we had our baths and made our way back down the basement stairs. Located against a wall as we descended the stairs was a pile of old, dusty, metal, miniature farm toys—little trucks and tractors, much past their prime and dotted with rust spots here and there. We dressed in our pajamas and made our way to the corner and started choosing toys to try out first.

That's when Walter's bedroom door opened.

He walked to the foot of the beds we had slept in the night before. The thought of bygones being bygones disappeared the second his hand went to the large buckle on his belt. Looking at John, he said, "I brought your piss-stained mattress back down here for you and I don't even get a 'thank you'?"

The whole time, that leather belt was making its way off his waist. We sat there and didn't move a muscle until John broke the silence.

"Thank you," he said in a quiet voice.

"Too late, pissant. Get on your feet, all three of you."

John slowly stood up. I remember hearing his knees pop. We followed suit and got to our feet as well. After what he had done to John that morning, I'd be fibbing if I said it did not completely terrify me at that moment. Walter folded the belt to where the buckle and end met and pushed both ends toward one another, allowing it to take on a smile, like a mouth gaping open. Then he pulled both ends outward in opposite directions and POP! POP! POP!

He snapped the belt three times.

"You three get your asses over here and lean over this bed."

I was already crying as we slowly walked toward this man, this full-grown man, and parked myself facedown as far away as I could locate myself from him. This happened to be the head of the bed by the stained pillows. I turned my face away from where Walter stood and from where John was, first in line. Jason was in the middle, then yours truly.

"Walter." A voice came from behind us and broke the terrifying anticipation of what was about to take place.

"Yeah, Ma?" he said.

Please stop him, please stop him, Carol.

"Hold on right there," she said.

Oh, Jesus, thank you, thank you a thousand times, thank you! The governor's calling, ladies and gentlemen, and we just got our last-minute reprieve.

"I'm not surprised you boys have little or no manners in public—or, should I say, our church," she said. My heart dropped. In a faraway, head in the clouds cooing, she continued, "Being raised by a drunken bastard and a crazy whore of a mother has certainly rubbed off on the three of you and stained you to the core."

POP! POP! POP!

I flinched, thinking Walter had started in on us.

"Our mom is not a whore and our dad isn't a bastard," John spoke.

Carol made her way over to where we lay, then leaned down and whispered, "That's the last time you talk back to me, boy. The very last time." Then, louder, she continued, "They failed you and your brothers and are the very reason you're here right now."

Jason and I, hearing this woman run our parents down, started crying. John, however, stood his ground.

"It's not our parents' fault that you shit kickers like hurting kids!"

"Walter," she said. "Please show this back-talking sinner what happens when you disrespect your betters."

Walter nodded, loading up with the belt before she stopped him, delaying the discipline.

"If he cries out, screams or makes one little sound, whip Jason and Joseph."

She floated up the basement stairs. John turned his head and looked at Jason and me. He looked pissed. It felt as though he wasn't so much pissed at them, though, but at us. It was as though he resented us for being there, like a burr under a saddle. Not only was his whooping imminent, but now he bore the full responsibility of curtailing the ass kicking we would receive if he so much as breathed heavily after each lash.

He lay forward across the bed, his butt facing outward on the edge of the bed, his head turned to the right, facing me and Jason.

Thwack!

John's eyes widened, and he clenched his teeth behind tightened lips.

Thwack!

Thwack!

Thwack!

These were not slow swings of the belt. Walter was really lacing into him. With each lash of the leather, John's face hardened and turned from pale to pink and, finally, red. When, at long last, their version of discipline ended, John had taken one for the team over twenty times. John didn't emit a single muffled cry or shaky hiccup. Not one sniffle. After Walter had finished with John, he turned his attention toward Jason and me. He walked over next to us and said, with a chuckle, "Your brother just saved your asses... literally."

John remained in the same position he had taken his whipping in for a minute, even after Walter, whistling as he went, had vacated the area. He slowly pushed himself from the bed up onto his unsteady feet. Now, you want to talk about beaming with pride? I know I damn sure was and I'll bet Jason was as well. No tears, no delayed sobbing, and no crumpling to the floor, body giving out after all that had just taken place. Not bad for a ten-year-old boy. It made what John said next hurt that much worse.

He looked at us two, vacancy in his chestnut brown eyes, and said, "I hate you."

He limped to the light switch and killed our source of illumination, walked back over to the bed that would become his nightly whipping post for the next year, and lay down, facing the basement wall.

At that moment, I believe that, deep in his heart and to the very core of his soul, he hated us and was wishing we'd never been born. He hadn't broken the way I'm sure they thought he would. However, inside, in his mind, his younger brothers had just become a burden.

Jason and I took to our bed stealth and silent, trying not to bother John or draw the ire of the piece of shit behind the door in the basement. Jason whispered to me before he rolled over and went to sleep.

"I think they're going to kill us."

A chill ran the length of my spine. It terrified me, laying there in that dark, musty basement. It's the only way I can describe how I felt. I was shaking, and it wasn't from being cold.

Our first twenty-four hours under the care of these bastards had thus concluded. The crazy counting at bath-time, followed up with a flyswatter assault upon arrival. John pissing the bed and getting the ass kicking reserved for most guys that have pinched the ass of someone's best gal at the local saloon. Almost being forced to hydrate ourselves with the rancid foot water of a bunch of crusty old guys after listening to Frank's rendition of two cats fucking in an alleyway. A ringing dinner bell and no invitation to eat any of the food prepared for this gaggle of assholes. John's second ass kicking of the day. Staving off his brothers' eventual meeting with Walter's belt by remaining as quiet as a church mouse during these worthless fucks' idea of reformation.

Some of the last words Virginia had said to us as we made our way to that small, Midwestern farmhouse had been: "This is your permanent foster home."

She may as well have told us it was to be our eternal hell.

It sure felt like it.

CHAPTER TEN

By the time Deputy Earl Alba, my personal ball-buster, fingerprints me and runs my social through NCIC, my testicles are at a dull roar.

"You ain't got a record, boy, but that don't mean shit to me."

Not wanting round two with old Earl, I remain silent.

"All the shit you was talking and now you ain't got nothing to say, smartass?"

His hand snaps out and vises onto my right shoulder. My blood flares like I'm thinking about doing something about it.

"That's enough, Earl."

The deputy's head whips around. His lips are still curled around the sneer he had been directing at me.

"No, sir! Not even close to being enough, Sheriff."

The sheriff stands about six-foot three and goes a svelte two hundred and twenty pounds, easily. He carries it well, unlike old Earl, whose gut is working overtime on the snaps that hold his two-toned tan and brown button-up together. He also looks cleaner, like his wife gives a damn about what she sends out into the world each day.

"We're all amped up, Deputy, understandably so, but the man has rights and we're going to treat him just as intended, understood?"

Old Earl lets go of my shoulder, shoving it backward as he does. "You didn't hear what he said to me, Sheriff. The little prick has more coming to him." Perhaps it is my imagination, but his voice seems to sound both sniveling and grunting. A hungry hog deprived of its meal was more pleasing to the ear than him.

The sheriff walks to where I'm sitting and looks down. I see his name plate.

"Thanks," I say. "Sheriff Luxemberg?"

"That's right. Gordon Luxemberg," he says.

"What kind of name is Luxemberg?"

"It's German, royal bloodlines—or so I was told."

Effectively, and mercifully, cut out of the conversation, Deputy Alba stalks off and plops down, defeated, in a worn, black, mesh-backed chair. It looks more comfortable than the wooden chair supporting my ass.

"Royalty. Wow, right here in the states. Where's your treasure? Or does the Baron send a monthly check?"

The sheriff flashes a grin at me, then looks back at his simmering deputy, laughing lightly, "He *is* a bit of a smartass, Earl."

"Look, Sheriff, I know my rights, even before he read them to me."

I look over at Mr. Mustache, but he ignores me. He just keeps cleaning his fingernails with a dull letter-opener, probably wishing he could bury it in me right about now. I look back to Sheriff Luxemberg.

"I did nothing to that man."

The sheriff rolls a chair over in front of me, seating himself at just above my eye level.

"You want out of them cuffs?" he asks.

I nod, all the while thinking, *What's the catch?*

"On your feet then, buddy."

I get up, face the wall, and, in moments, am sitting back down, rubbing my wrists and, with a quick grimace, adjusting the water gun and balloons. The deputy grins, nice and ugly. I scowl right back at him. Sheriff Luxemberg overlooks the exchange. After settling, I ask, "How's John?"

The sheriff frowns. "He's calmed down and closed up shop."

I frown right back. That doesn't sound like John. At least, not the John I had known for a long time now.

"I figured the way he was giving you all what-for on the way in, he'd still be looking to scrap," I say.

"I figured about the same," the Sheriff says. Then he eyes me. "We know you did nothing."

I'm sure he sees the shock on my face. Declaring my innocence so quick, just as an investigation was getting under way, is surprising, especially since I had been on the scene at the time the fat bastard had given up the ghost. This time, I ask right out, "What's the catch, Sheriff?"

"No catch," he says. "The wife, shaken as she is, told a deputy on the scene you showed up and tried to stop your brother. She told him you backed her off the stairs, otherwise she might have fallen under the barrel of, and I quote, 'that son of a whore that murdered my husband'."

Now, where have I heard that phrase before?

"We saw you drop to your knees through the front door when we were closing in on you and I could've sworn I heard you tell your brother he could 'take off' and 'not do this', in so many words."

"Why the cuffs and the free ride with Barney over there, Sheriff?"

"Barney" looks over, glaring, and his short, pudgy middle-finger springs to life.

I jeer back at him. "Is that the size of your little cornstalk, jag off?"

He shoots to his feet, chair banging the wall, pointy object still in hand.

"Earl, goddammit, get out of here!" the sheriff bellows. Then, just a mite quieter, but not less stern, "I got this."

Earl slings the opener to the vulcanized desk-top with a slight tinging sound.

"I hope your crazy-ass brother catches fire when they light him up, little prick."

He huffs out through the back door, attempting to slam it as hard as he can. Much like his life, he fails miserably, denied by the pneumatic piston that allows it to lock in place after a few seconds.

"You'll have to forgive him. He knew the deceased well, so you can understand his frame of mind," the sheriff says.

"He must not know him too well. If he did, he might decide to pin a medal on my brother right now," I shoot back.

Even reeling from the murder committed before my eyes, I can't help but feel relief. That part of me that never moved on, just like that part in John, had always needed this moment to come to pass. I'm reveling in that monster's death, even as the rest of me sits here pleading my innocence.

He sits silently for a moment or two, absorbing what I said. "Suppose you enlighten me, buddy," he finally says.

"What do you wanna know?" I ask.

"Well, for starters, how did your brother know the man? Through cattle auctions or his farm, maybe?"

The farm, the cattle, the year we spent with him and his family, the devil in every single one of them, I think. *Where to start?*

CHAPTER ELEVEN

The second morning with the Ward family was almost an exact duplicate of the first morning. The difference was, Jason had pissed the bed that morning, so he replaced John as the recipient of Walter's rage, belt, boots, and verbal assault. This time around, however, during the utter annihilation of Jason's ass, he passed out after several hard—and I mean *hard*—kicks to his ass and lower back. I'm telling you, he passed out cold.

Jason began snoring, as though he were sleeping. The sound startled all of us. Walter stopped kicking. He settled into instant panic mode. His facial expression went from pure anger and hate to *oh shit, I may have just kicked this kid to death!* He poked Jason with the tip of his cowboy boot.

"Wake up, boy."

Nothing.

"I said wake up."

Jason snored.

"Wake up!"

Walter was now rubbing the back of Jason's thigh with the heel of his boot. Jason finally moved his body around a little. His hands curled into little claws, and he pulled his knees up to his chest. His eyes fluttered open, then closed, opened, then closed. Finally, they remained open, but just barely.

"Get up, boy. C'mon now, get up," Walter stammered, wiping his brow with the back of his arm.

After Jason got up and appeared no worse for the wear, Walter made him drag the mattress across the floor and up the stairs the same way he had made John do it. Then he told us to get cleaned up real quick and get ready to head out to do the same chores as we had the morning before.

A lot of these abuses ended up happening every other day, if not almost daily—especially when it came to bed-wetting. Jason had a bit of a bed-wetting issue even at home, before foster care. John, though, had rarely, if ever, had accidents back home. But after that first and second morning of ass whoopings, John became leakier.

Jason may as well have been Old Faithful. Every time one of them wet the bed, the physical and verbal abuse got worse. You'd think that fat, dumb bastard would have realized and maybe even thought to himself, *Hey, these ass kickings* and *the whole name-calling barrage do not seem to have the effect I'm trying to achieve.*

But if he ever had any sort of revelation, he didn't act on it. And so, after each episode, whether it be one of my brothers, or both, the dumbass would beat the crap out of them, only to find their night-time relief problems becoming more and more frequent. Was he blue-collar smart? You bet. A regular midwestern mechanical magician, that one. He could fix this and rig that to make just about anything work.

The oaf never once caught on. Maybe it was getting worse with every other over-the-top ass kicking he administered. The way I saw it, the two of them were like Pavlov's dogs. Walter was the bell and John and Jason were the hungry pups. Their heads hit the pillows and, much like canines slobbering all over themselves, my brothers' floodgates opened and they pissed all over the place, starving for a moment's peace with nowhere to hide.

Then, one morning, I awoke and things were a little different. I was warm, but also cold. My clothes were wet and freezing. My skin stuck to the sheets, feeling tacky and dirty. During the night, I must have cut loose with a lot of pee and was now soaked to the skin in urine. I became filled with terror and dread. I jumped up and tried desperately to remove my clothes.

Maybe I could shove them under the bed? But what about the sheets? How would I explain away my lack of clothes? What about the smell?

My mind scrambled for a plan to hide what I had done before it was too late. But, like clockwork, Walter came out of his room before I decided. I watched in slow motion as he saw what I had done and almost seemed to light up with glee at having a new target. My heart dropped. I knew what came next.

He ripped into me like he had my brothers, just like I knew he would. I knew he would kick me. I knew he would beat me with his belt. Even knowing that, it did not prepare me for how he kicked me so hard it felt like my spine had pushed up through my skull and lodged in place there. I hadn't expected the way I couldn't breathe. Every time I'd get a brief whisper of air into my lungs, he would kick the precious oxygen right back out.

It was like a bastardized strangling, a suffocation the likes of which I could never have imagined. This was how I was going to die. This was how one of us was going to die.

After a good amount of kicks and cracks from the belt, Walter backed off. I woke up from the foggy state of consciousness my lack of air had dropped me into. Following the same instructions as my brothers, I had to drag that mattress up the stairs and out that door. Along the route, Walter kicked me in the ass and legs and berated me with the usual monikers he'd assigned to John and Jason, like "pissant" and "sinner". He called me a "little fucking pecker-head". That was new to me. I hadn't yet heard that one from him, so I guess he was probably saving that one for me once I finally screwed up.

Once my personal ass kicking from him was over, I found myself back in the basement with both of my brothers, getting ready for the morning. My crying subsided after a while when I realized that the round was over and I was alive and kicking. I had never pissed the bed before. I wondered what had triggered me peeing the bed.

The answer was: not a single thing. I had used the bathroom right up to the minute we had to be in the basement, like I had always done before bedtime. Later, down the road, Jason came clean with me. He had done it. He had pissed the bed.

"When I woke up, and I realized what I had done, I crawled over you and nudged you across the bed, on top of the accident."

He confessed he allowed me to take the blame because he was so beat up and scared he didn't think he could take anymore.

"You never took a beating for pissing the bed," he justified.

"Why didn't you say something? He was kicking the crap out of me."

Jason, in the way only he could, looked at me and said, "I froze in fear and shame that I did that to you, but you hadn't gotten your piss-the-bed ass whooping yet. I was sort of happy it was you and not me for once."

Looking back on it, I wish I could've told Jason at the time that there was no need to feel shame and that I wasn't mad. The way I came to see it, if I took one beating away from him or John, I was glad I could contribute to the team. No apology necessary.

CHAPTER TWELVE

Prior to our arrival, the Wards had enrolled us at Ridgeway Elementary School. My classes took place in a large mobile trailer by the playground while my brothers were in the actual elementary building. On the very first day, I made friends pretty quick with some boys in my class. I experienced no type of bullying or crossway glances from any of my classmates. It was a seamless transition. *Thank God*. I took pride in my advanced reading skills, enjoying the quiet reading time in the library like Beethoven on a piano.

In a short time, I also developed a bit of a crush on a little strawberry-blonde gal named Amanda. One day at recess, me and the rest of the boys had a pretty physical game of capture-the-flag. The fair maidens cheered on their favorite combatant from the side of the open, grassy area we had designated our kingdoms. Here I proved to all the boys I was a formidable force to be reckoned with. Having made the best progress against my enemies, my queen awaited me by the tower—a red and yellow slide. Amanda rewarded me with my first kiss. To the victor went the spoils, and I was on cloud nine, to say the very least.

While I basked in the glory of my academic and physical accomplishments at school, my brothers withdrew and found it hard to make friends. They stood off on the sidelines during our recess games and watched, disinterested and aching. Their quiet and somber faces of dread warded away kids who were curious enough to approach. Their grades suffered, too. They paid little attention in class, their minds being on more important matters such as pain, and their performance showed it.

After several weeks of sporadic bed-wetting and feeling Walter's wrath, their days became consumed with thoughts of what awaited them when our school-bus arrived back at the house.

Walter had transitioned to dishing out his punishment, seventy-five percent of the time, after he had finished a hard day at work. Some men get home from a hard day at the office and relieve their stress by either having a nice adult beverage over ice or a little nicotine from a pipe or a smoke. Walter took the edge off at the expense of John and Jason's asses. If there was an accident that morning, they would stew all day at school, knowing what lay ahead of them, unable to concentrate on their school-work. Then we would return from school and sit in that basement, with its ground-level, horizontal windows that faced the driveway. It was the worst part of the day.

When Walter's truck tires came into view, the color in one, if not all, of our faces drained away and our insides turned to jelly.

T-Minus sixty seconds and counting.

That was around the stomping distance and time it took Walter to get from his truck to the back door. Then his loud bellowing would begin. While he was descending the stairs, he'd already be pulling his belt from around his waist. Even if I didn't witness it, I could hear his verbal and physical assault booming throughout the house.

I was safe from most of those beatings because I had established myself as a child who seemed to hold his liquid at night. Jason and John not so much. It was difficult to watch or, if I was upstairs, hear it happen repeatedly.

While my brothers were getting theirs downstairs, I was often getting mine upstairs at the hands of Carol or Arthur for what became my weakness: warm cow milk, either by the glass or mixed with that morning's malt-o-meal. I could not stand the warmth of that milk coming straight out of the beast. I would involuntarily gag, trying to finish what I had been served. Most of the time, I could not finish it at all.

Food was "not to be wasted in this house, boy!"

I'd come home from school and the warm cup of milk or, even worse, a congealed bowl of malt-o-meal mixed with milk I hadn't finished that morning would be waiting for me on the small table in the kitchen.

Now, Carol wouldn't throw it in the refrigerator and then have me pick up where I had left off that morning. No. Instead, whatever I could not stomach upon awakening would sit out where I had left it. The milk would slightly sour and, when it was mixed, a thick skin would form on the top with a gelatinous, fermented goop underneath.

"You're going to finish it and you had better not try to throw it out or throw it up," she would say.

So, with my task laid out before me, I'd either sip or nibble at that shit. When I could stomach a small portion, I'd begin heaving and gagging and up it would come, right back into the bowl. Carol or Arthur—usually, it was Carol—would have me go into the dining room and lean over a chair and then they would strap the hell out of me with a belt.

Facing the same situation as I had before, I'd devised a master plan. When Carol walked away from my very own foul-food court, I'd rush downstairs and throw the remnants of punishment in the dog bowl. On more than one occasion, I got away with it. Most of the time, she'd stand guard, making sure her wasteful ward of the state finished what he'd started.

I would know that morning on my way to school what acrid doom was awaiting me that afternoon, but, for one reason or another, I wouldn't dwell on it the way my brothers did. It hurt like hell when I'd get strapped. But I knew firsthand Walter had a lot more power behind every swing of the belt than his parents. And, let's not forget, Walter loved to kick.

If you would have placed a tape recorder in that house and played it back before bed, you would hear the cries of three small boys about every other night. There was laughter in that house, too, but it never came from my brothers or me. After a while, it seems, we just forgot how to laugh regardless of what was taking place.

CHAPTER THIRTEEN

"What do you say? Can I see him?"

Luxemburg doesn't act surprised at the question. From the look on his tanned face, one might think he was already considering it. He doesn't answer, though. He stands up and walks toward the chugging, white-and-green coffee pot.

"Leaded or unleaded?" he asks.

"Unleaded. Fill it up, Sheriff."

I'd given up the stuff about five years prior after the beverage had me running to the can after a single serving. But if ever there was a time to brighten my senses, this would be it.

He returns with a full, black coffee in a stained, tan mug, no doubt the community cup. There are no police logos or #1 dad mugs for me. He eases down in his chair and blow soft across the top of his beverage, steam wafting toward me.

"You know, friend—can I call you friend?"

"Call me what you like, just don't call me John."

His response to that is a simple "hmm". He takes a long pull from the top of his cup, the liquid still piping hot. "Damn! That java is like lava," he says, fanning his open mouth.

I wait, hanging in the moment. Finally, the interior of his pie-hole cools and he gets back to the subject. "You know, friend, ask any man around here and they'll tell you we like to keep things in-house. When something like this happens—which up to now was damn near never—we take it personal." He takes the time to breathe in deep and then continues, "The state people will be here and they'll take over and start waffle stomping the shit out of what little we've accomplished."

I get where he's coming from to a certain degree. Every dog with a backyard of his own has a favorite spot to piss and most take offense to a bigger dog coming over and doing his business over their puddle.

"What do you need me to do, Sheriff?"

His head bobs up and down, considering the question.

"Well, I could take you back to see if you can unhinge his jaw some, if that's something you're comfortable with, buddy."

"He won't say a damn word if you're back there with me. I know his ways, Sheriff. He won't." I'm only partially bluffing. The John the sheriff is talking about is a different beast than what I'm used to. The man that had pulled that trigger wasn't my brother anymore, from every fucked-up avenue one could muster.

He sips and thinks about it. "Well, I can probably swing that if you think you might persuade him to make a simple statement—you know, just enough to—"

I cut him off. "'Incriminate himself?'"

"Not what I was going to say, friend."

He seems mildly irritated.

"Look, Sheriff, I can't guarantee anything. It's not as though either of us has been through this before. I may squeeze his reasonings for why he did what he did, but it will not vary much, I guarantee you that."

His mood lightens again. "That's all I'm trying for, friend. A simple why, something to give the big boys when they get here. I can relay your conversation to them," he says. The tone of his voice shows that there is a 'but' coming. "But they'd rather hear it came from that Wyatt Earp wannabe in there."

"If John and I are alone, how's that gonna help you? The information would still be second hand."

He smiles, close-mouthed. "I know we're just a small-town cop shop but you're in meth and weed country. If you think I can't listen in and record audio of conversation, you'd be wrong. Users and dealers talk when badges aren't present and, sometimes, a little inadvertent rambling can point a good man in the right direction, help keep things squeaky clean and John Q. happy."

Sounds illegal to me, but I'm no lawyer, so maybe it isn't. Who the hell am I to question his methods if it kept Farmer Ken and Jane smiling over the morning paper and their scrambled eggs?

"You got a deal. I'll see what I can pull out of him," I say.

He gets up and walks toward the wall between us and the bad guys.

"How long should I wait to start asking questions?"

He reaches the wall and flips a silver toggle switch upward and turns a dial all the way to the right, then looks over his shoulder. "When your tongue crosses the doorjamb, let the words flow like a frigging river."

I get up, and he walks me to the door that leads to my brother. I take a deep breath. Luxemburg keys the door and, one loud, metallic clunk later, fluorescent light fills my vision. Just to the left, in the three-cell jail, sits John. He looks up, and, for a split second, his brown eyes look pure black. Had I not known him, I'd have thought him to be the devil himself, tricked and trapped by mortal man.

Biding his time.

Ready.

Waiting.

CHAPTER FOURTEEN

A s the weeks wore on, the temperatures outside rose and winter gave way to early spring. The three of us boys started getting used to the daily grind of chores, school, home, begging, pleading, belts, boots, crying, bed, chores. After a while, I moved upstairs and slept in the same room as my foster brother, Robbie. I had earned a spot in his room for not being a bedwetter. John and Jason remained in the basement and were never, not one time, allowed upstairs after lights out. It was like I had moved up into purgatory while my brothers stayed in hell, kept under the steadfast guard of Walter the demon.

The sun had been staying out longer, so we often escaped to the great outdoors. At some point, Jason dug around in the basement and came across an old, oversized, red plastic bat and three wiffle balls. Along with Robbie, the three of us formed a makeshift baseball diamond in the backyard. Home plate was at the edge of the driveway, where the grass met the dirt and gravel. First base was a wooden post with a small light attached to the top of it, second base was an old frisbee, and third was a bare spot on the ground where grass refused to grow.

To my surprise, we could usually play just like we had at home, batting, pitching, and fielding in turns without interruption or punishment for making too much noise or having too much fun. This was a welcome relief, and we enjoyed it for as long as we could and as often as we could. The little spoiled prince, Robbie, would sometimes get frustrated if he was pitching and one of us got extra base hits off him.

"Chuh, chuh, chuh" would come from his mouth as one of us rounded first and headed to second.

He would bitch and moan for a minute, threaten to quit playing, and then recant and keep right on pitching. I think he enjoyed having us boys to play with because his siblings were adults and had no time for such nonsense or, as with his brother Douglas, who had just started college, were just absent.

These spirited games of wiffle ball usually took place on evenings when all of us boys had stayed out of the crosshairs of those that doled out punishment. Hell, if by some miracle we all stayed dry overnight, ate or drank all of our food, and said nothing to piss them off, it ended up being a fun night. Walter would pull up in his truck, exit the vehicle, and, without a glance at any of us, head into the house and disappear for the evening.

Some nights, Carol and Arthur would pull up a chair and watch us play from the back stoop. Those nights were few, but very much welcomed when we got them. One night, believe it or not, Walter even waddled his fat ass out to the rock we substituted as the rubber for the pitcher's mound and lobbed slow, arcing balls, better than Robbie could pitch. We'd hit, run, and play. Why couldn't he be like this instead of the bastard he almost always was?

I remember being at bat and him tossing a nicely placed ball right down the middle. I swung and drove that ball over everybody's head and made it to third standing up and then home on a throwing error.

Walter chirped, "Look at Killer Kowalski go!"

He let me bat again, out of order, and again I drove the ball deep to what would be centerfield and almost touched them all again.

"Old Killer Kowalski!" he exclaimed.

I didn't know who the hell Killer Kowalski was, and I didn't care. It was praise, actual praise, from this man who was usually so filled with hate. It could have or should have stayed like that. Later I learned Killer Kowalski had been a professional wrestler. The moron didn't know household names like Stargell or Fisk?

But then leave it to Walter to ruin what little fun we'd been having.

One evening, we were outside having ourselves a nice game. He pulled up in his truck, came to a stop, got out, and slammed his door, grumbling all the way to the house. None of us had done anything that warranted him getting after us but, naturally, when he was in a mood, it usually meant bad news for one, if not all of us. We warily watched him disappear into the house. When he didn't return right away, we went back to our game of ball, relieved.

It was my turn at bat, and Robbie lobbed a nice one to me. I got all of it and headed toward the light post, touched it with my hand, and sped away toward second base. My foot brushed the frisbee, and I turned and headed for third. That's when my ass started burning, the way it feels when you get stung by a bee or a wasp. I stopped in my tracks and reached back and grasped at my right ass cheek. Simultaneously, I heard a light pop and felt more stinging on the back of my right thigh. I cried as I spun around to see what the hell was biting me, only to find Walter, sitting on the back stoop, pumping up a pellet rifle and smiling at me all the while.

I did not know what kind of gun it was, having never seen a pellet rifle, but what I knew was that the bastard had shot me and, from the looks of it, he was taking aim again!

I took off. Pop! He hit me right in the same cheek as before and I dropped to the ground. The waterworks were in full force and John, Jason, and, yes, even Robbie were scrambling for cover.

"You better get to home plate, Killer Kowalski!" he called, pumping that damn gun up again.

Rushing to my feet, and hauling ass to the driveway, I heard the pop sound from the pellet rifle. Luckily for me, this time he missed. I scurried toward a pile of branches to take cover with the other boys. The prick was laughing.

Tears were flowing pretty well now. Walter hollered, "It's just a pellet gun, you little baby!"

I rubbed the spots on my ass and leg and he yelled, "I thought Killer Kowalski was tough!"

He took aim again, and we ducked for cover. The pellet ricocheted through the branches and missed us. Then, he stood up and shouted for us to come back out. We didn't move, so he yelled louder, "I said get your asses back over here!"

All four of us did as we were told, making our way back into the yard.

Robbie hauled ass toward the front of the house and disappeared out of sight, going "chuh, chuh, chuh" the entire way.

"Line up," Walter said, all the while pumping more air into that fucking pellet gun.

All three of us lined up. Then he instructed each of us to take off, one at a time, across the backyard. The bastard looked surprised when we just stood there, frozen on the spot.

"I said move, boy," he directed at John, who had taken the lead in line, as usual.

John looked at Jason and me and instructed, "Run as fast as you can. Don't slow down, even if he hits you."

Walter screamed, "Move!"

John took off, parallel to the back stoop, and Walter took aim. The barrel of the rifle slowly followed John from right to left. The aerated familiar pop sounded. He missed. John made it to the other side of the backyard.

"You lucky little pissant!" he yelled. Then he turned his attention to Jason, again filling the pellet rifle up with air. "Move."

Jason took off. Pop! This time, the projectile found its mark dead center on Jason's left hip. He howled in pain but did as John said and limped the rest of the way across the yard while Walter, with great delight, pumped up the rifle. Then Walter looked at me and motioned with his head to the left, meaning for me to begin my run. I took off and, halfway across the yard, I heard the pop, but felt no sting. *Whew!* I made it to the other side with my brothers. Jason was crying and rubbing his hip.

"Line up!" Walter hollered again while funneling more pellets into the rifle.

By the time we finished running Walter's gauntlet, he had popped each of us a few times. We were panting and trembling from the pain and exhaustion.

The sun was setting, and it was getting dark. Carol emerged from the house.

"Walter, stop playing with them boys. It's dinnertime."

Playing? Well, I guess if you've had a bad day... I remember thinking bitterly.

And to think this delusional bastard and his family were being paid by the state of Kansas to sharpen his shooting skills with a fucking child's first gun. When we made our way inside, I went to the bathroom and could twist my torso around enough to see around eight to ten purple and red welts about the size of the letter O on a computer keyboard.

The bit of joy we had experienced that early spring playing wiffle ball was over, stripped away by that fat oaf and his idea of fun and games.

Walter giveth and Walter taketh away.

CHAPTER FIFTEEN

Spring had sprung and, seeing as how the fun of our little ball game had been ruined, we found ourselves, more often than not, wandering up the dirt road in front of the house, toward the old church that sat on the corner at the top of the hill and the cemetery behind it. Once there, we three boys would wonder around the old gravestones and markers, reading the names of the people that had passed many years before. Sometimes we would climb an enormous tree in the middle of the plots.

From there, we could see Walter approaching from a respectful distance in his truck and knew he couldn't see us. If he couldn't find us, he would leave us alone. Out of sight, out of mind. The cemetery felt like it was as safe a place as any to avoid the foster parents and Walter. Not to mention, we were feeling like the living dead, so why not hang out with those that were already departed?

Moments of peace like that were few though, and it only took a morning's drive out to the pasture to put shit back into perspective. We were in the back of the truck kicking hay off to the hungry cows as usual one particular morning when Walter, being the sadistic prick that he was, crept slow along a fence line and, after a while, came to a stop to check the condition of some fencing that was installed to keep the cows and the four horses on their separate sides of the pasture.

"Climb on down, boys," he called back to us.

Great, now what? I thought.

He pointed to some tall stalks of brightly colored, trashy-looking weeds and instructed us to grab them at the base and pull them up by the root.

"Make sure and get all of it out of the ground," he said.

When we jerked them out of the earth, the exposed root of each clump was white and wet. He watched us work for a while. Then, getting bored, he stopped us and had some fun at our expense.

"Jason, take that root and lay the end across that fence wire."

Jason did as he was told. But as he went through with the command, his hand snapped back quickly and Walter started laughing. It was an electric fence that Jason had touched the white, wet root to and it gave him a bit of a shock in his right hand. It wasn't enough to hurt him, more surprising than anything else. Walter then had John do it.

"Tickles," John said, jumping back and dropping his handful of roots to the ground.

"Go ahead," Walter said to me.

Timid, I reached forward with the clump. Upon contact, I felt an immediate tingle go up my right arm and I released my handful as well. We all just stood there. After a minute, John said, "Can I try it again?"

"Sure, go ahead," Walter said. We should've suspected his easygoing nature.

John did it again, then Jason, then me.

"See who can hold it there the longest," Walter suggested.

In the spirit of competition, we did. One of us would make contact while the other two counted out Mississippis, arguing with one another after each turn.

"You were counting slower for me."

"I'm winning, you gotta beat four."

"Okay, now beat five."

After we had finished, and we declared John the champion by a narrow margin over Jason, Walter said, "Hold on, boys. I gotta take a leak."

He did his business, then turned to us and said, "If any of you gotta piss, do it now."

We walked behind the truck to do just that. Walter stopped us and said, "Nuh uh, not there. Piss on that fence." A small smile lurked under his thick mustache.

I no longer had the urge to go and my testicles crawled up inside my body upon this fucked up directive. "I don't have to," I said.

His smile evaporated, replaced with a frown.

"All three of you had to piss a second ago. Are you liars?"

That was the last word we wanted him flinging at us. We never liked what came next.

We made our way over to the fence, one by one, starting with me since I opened my mouth first and had recanted. I pulled out the old mushroom cap and felt the cool morning breeze trigger the urge to urinate.

I thought, *If I put this off as long as I can, maybe it won't be so bad.* After all, it didn't really hurt my hand or arm.

What I didn't realize at the time was that the weeds were just wet, creating a small amount of conduction. But urine? Urine is ninety-five percent water, no big deal. The other five percent, though, comprising of uric acid and salt, makes a world of difference. This combination turns that stream of piss into a conductive superhighway.

I let loose with a solid jet of lightly hued yellow piss. When it contacted that wire, nothing happened.

At first.

Then, it felt as though my entire body had locked up. A bolt of pain shot through my lower regions unlike anything I had ever felt before. Most young men have had a moment where an accidental shot to the nuts while wrestling or just playing happens. But this wicked sensation that knocked me on my ass and caused me to piss on myself was way worse. It was like someone had stuck a hot metal rod into my guts through my outbound lane. I writhed around on the ground, sweat forming on my forehead and piss soaking my pant legs. My brothers, fearful but obedient, followed suit and, hoping for the best but receiving the worst, ended up on the ground writhing in agony right along with me.

Meanwhile, Walter was as tickled as pigs in shit, just laughing his fat ass off, tears welling up behind his stupid, tinted prescription glasses.

"Get up and get on the truck, ya babies," he said. "I thought you boys were tougher than that." Then his laughter died down and the familiar, dark and brooding look reappeared on his smug face.

"I thought a real badass raised you peckerwoods?"

He shook his head and ambled toward the truck. "Your dad must be a real pussy," he said as he slid into the truck and waited for us to crawl aboard.

Great, another verbal jab at our dad. He wouldn't've been saying that if he was face to face with our old man. If our dad knew what he had just done, the fat piece of shit would have never made it out of that pasture in one piece—or breathing.

That latter of the two scenarios would have suited me just fine.

CHAPTER SIXTEEN

As the days got warmer, we also learned that our foster family ran not one but two lumberyards. One was in Ridgeway, Kansas, operated by their vocally challenged son, Frank. The other was in a town a little northwest of the Ridgeway location called Grander. This was where Arthur and Carol would spend most of their workdays.

In the spirit of spring cleaning, they got us boys out of the house by putting us to work at Frank's store. So, every day after school, while our classmates were playing outside and enjoying the change in weather, they instructed us to walk the short distance to Frank's store and help there.

They taught us how to sort and pick lumber for customers as their orders came in. We learned the difference between a two-by-four and a two-by-six and, after a short time, learned how to weigh nails. We also learned the differences in sixteen penny, eight penny, and finish nails. It wasn't a bad gig, and it got us away from the house most afternoons, so not an awful racket. We received no pay for our duties because child labor wasn't legal. They wouldn't have wanted to break the law, what with them being such upstanding citizens and always having a child's best interest at heart.

One day, Carol was at the Ridgeway location, and she asked me the time. I looked at the clock. It may as well have been Chinese characters.

I hadn't yet learned to put together the big and little hands on the clock to come up with the proper time.

"Well, we will just have to fix that, kiddo. My gosh, didn't your parents teach you anything?"

She gasped as though me failing to learn to tell time would end the world. The old bat ignored my glare and continued, "I'm not surprised, what with a crazy loon and drunk taking care of you."

Ah, yes, another day, another jab at our parents. Par for the course.

She sat me down in a wooden chair facing the wall clock and explained how the tiny, stick-like hand goes around every sixty seconds, which comprised one minute, and then the long hand would click over to the next minute. After sixty revolutions of the long hand, the short, fat hand would move to the next large numeral on the clock face, and that totaled an hour. She took the clock off the wall and turned it to different times and quizzed me. This went on for a couple of days and, before I knew it, I was telling time like nobody's business.

Thank you, Carol. Now I could tell what time the lumberyard closed, or, at school, how close recess was and, when back at the farm, what time I got my ass beat while lying over a dining room chair facing their grandfather clock.

It made it easier to anticipate the finer things in life.

Hey, it gonged six times. Time for a good old-fashioned ass whooping.

One day after school, Frank met us in the main storefront and told us we had been doing a pretty good job and, if we kept it up, soon our reward would be a Barlow brand pocketknife. He sold them out of a glass display case to customers looking for that special lumberyard impulse item upon check out. We wouldn't get one to share, mind you, but one for each of us. Sweet!

We hustled the orders out as fast as customers could place their request. Lumber was loaded or staged for specific cut lengths. We weighed nails and placed them in brown paper bags. It was great. Talk about incentive. During down time, we'd peer through the glass case and pointed at which one we liked. This went on for several days and, feeling closer to our goal every day, we worked with increasing enthusiasm as the days went on.

One afternoon, Frank came around the back corner of the lumber storage building. He walked at a rather brisk pace in our direction, where we were waiting to fill any order that might come our way. His face was beet red, and he looked angry. This was not normal for him. He had been nothing but a calm, level-headed person so far. He got to where we were standing and leaned down and said, "Which one of you thieving little bastards stole a knife out from up front?"

We looked at each other, pissed off and thinking, *Why would you do that and ruin everything?*

"Turn out your pockets right now, you little bastards," he growled. His voice took on the familiar tone, just like the rest of his family.

We did and, as usual, there was nothing but lint produced from the bottom of our Tough-Skin pockets.

"One of you hid it somewhere and you better go get it right now or your ass is grass!"

Not one of us took a step in any direction as we began denying in unison that we had stolen nothing. Frank walked over to a sawhorse in the cutting room and brought it back out into the bright sunlight.

"All three of you, lean over this right now!" he boomed. I felt a part of me become resigned to the explosion we were watching take place in front of our faces.

In hindsight, it would have only been a matter of time before he soured against our existence, just like the rest of them. Positioning my upper half over the sawhorse, I was already tensing up, following my brother's lead in his commitment to punishment. He then picked up a one-by-four and beat our asses with it. All the while, we were pleading our case through a waterfall of tears. He'd pause, ask again, and, when no resolution to the problem presented itself, rip into us with enthusiastic energy.

"Tell me where that knife is, you little bastards!"

Just when we'd had about as much as a guy can take, a voice came from behind us, yelling, "Stop! *Stop!* I did it! *I took it!*"

It was Thomas, Frank's girlfriend's young boy. Apparently, he had been listening from over by the trailer the three of them occupied, just a short distance from the backside of the lumberyard. Frank stopped the thrashing he was putting on us and turned to the boy.

"What?" he asked. "Why?"

The little boy, through his tears, informed Frank that after hearing that we were going to get a knife, well, he wanted one too and, with no way to earn one for himself, he simply took one while the front was slow and no one was within view.

"I'm sorry, Frank. I'm sorry, I'm sorry!" Thomas cried.

Frank dropped the piece of lumber and squatted down in front of Thomas and put his arms around him. "It's okay. Calm down, Thomas. It's okay. You told the truth, that's all that matters."

That's all that matters? The truth was all that mattered?

That fucking prick! We had been telling him the truth, but it didn't seem to matter much to him as he welted our asses with that stick of lumber! He walked Thomas, who was almost inconsolable, back toward the trailer to retrieve the missing pocketknife. There was no apology, no "oops, sorry, my bad", not a goddamn bit of remorse for the mistake he had made. He didn't even bring it up after he had come back and placed the filched knife in the display case. He just sent us back to work.

After that, he no longer praised our efforts and was distant from us. Maybe he felt bad for what he did, I'm not sure. I know I would have felt like a piece of shit. The promise of new pocketknives for all our efforts disappeared.

We never ended up getting them.

CHAPTER SEVENTEEN

It was a bright, beautiful March weekend when me and my brothers met Douglas. He was the fifth child and had been away attending college. We had been playing in the yard, blissful and free from the scrutinizing eyes inside the house. The crunch of tires on gravel first signaled his arrival.

We looked up, surprised, expecting to see Walter's beat-up truck coming home early. But this was a used, green Mercury Comet. We had never seen it before. But it was clear this person was no stranger to the farm.

It sped up the drive faster than allowed, turning and swerving around the potholes with an intimate familiarity that sent shivers of dread down our spine. This was another member of the family coming home, a stranger that would enjoy nothing more than to join in on heaping pain on us boys.

A jolly fellow exploded out of the car and on to the scene. The young man looked like the rest of his family. He guy sported the ever-present tinted glasses, possibly purchased in bulk. He resembled Walter more than the other family members. He was a little overweight and wore a "Keep On Trucking" tank top with a thick leather belt keeping his ass in his jeans.

For all that he was similar, you could also spot the differences between him and his brothers. He had a smile that could light up a dark room and he carried himself with that carefree, youthful enthusiasm young men often do, not the scowl Walter wore. He bounded toward us like a new baby foal, off-balance and over-exaggerated in every step he took.

"Well, hey, guys," he said. "I'm Douglas. And who the heck are you?"

With caution, we introduced ourselves, not sure what to make of this larger-than-life fellow.

"How long have you been here?" he asked, smiling at us the whole time, eyes darting from one to the next.

We shrugged and then he did something that made us feel human again for the first time in a long time.

He hugged each of us.

And it wasn't just any hug, but a big old bear hug. It enveloped all three of us. In an instant, we trusted this young man. And before stepping inside to say hello to his biological family, he did one better. His eyes squinted behind his glasses, and he looked around at us, his head kind of comical, lolling back and forth.

"I feel like cruising around a little more and I got one important question. Are you prisoners breaking out of this jail with me?"

Before we knew it, he had us in that old Mercury and we were backing out of the driveway and heading down the road, dust flying up behind us, his radio blaring "Detroit Rock City" by Kiss, and wheels turning much too fast for the loose dirt and gravel that made up the surface. We had escaped, if only for a little while, compliments of Douglas. When we arrived back at the farm, Carol scolded Douglas for taking off with us and he apologized in an over-the-top way that only he could and then, before following her through the door, he turned toward us, rolled his eyes, and gave us a quick wink and a smile.

We had to ask ourselves... who in the hell raised this young man? Was it the same people that kept us on a steady diet of mental, verbal, and physical abuse? Did he get dropped off by some alien life form or escape from the circus?

No. Somehow, someway, he was part of the same family that did those horrible things. Something about him made him different, made him who he was as a person, different from the rest.

He had compassion, and he had a conscience and, most of all, he had a heart. Douglas treated us with dignity. Douglas treated us with respect. He threw in that dose of compassion with a shot of comedy that made us feel like there was a light at the end of the tunnel. Our seclusion out there on that farm had turned our world topsy-turvy, but Douglas had helped us believe again that good people were still out there. He brought an emotion and a word back into our lives we feared we'd lost forever.

Hope.

But anything that entered our lives that was decent and pure never lasted.

It seemed as quick as Douglas had arrived, he was getting ready to leave, what with being a busy college student and all. Before he left that Sunday afternoon, he overheard a conversation between John and Robbie. John had noticed Robbie gearing up to take a ride on his dirt bike and he was asking–begging–Robbie for a ride on the back of it.

Per usual, Robbie denied John the simple pleasure of a ride down the road to the corner and back to the house. It would have taken him a couple of minutes at the most to complete a minor act of kindness. Being kind wasn't Robbie's strong suit. He kicked the bike to life and sped away without a second glance or thought. He was a little prick.

John, defeated and disappointed, the norm for the three of us, walked back to where Jason and I were laying in the grass, staring up at clusters of slow-moving clouds. Having no toys of our own to play with, we would often just lay down, stare up at the sky, and imagine up a better world for ourselves. Something as simple as a cloud could slowly morph into the head of a horse, or two boats adrift on the ocean, colliding.

"That one looks like a hand."

"No, it looks like Pike's Peak."

John sat down and leaned on the grass next to us. "He's a jerk face," he stated.

No arguments here, buddy.

A few minutes passed, and Douglas hollered at us from the opening at the side of the barn. "Hey, guys! What do you think?"

As we sat up and looked in his direction, Douglas emerged from the doorway, pushing an old, dusty motorized minibike out to the driveway.

"Let's see if we can get this puppy started!" he exclaimed.

We sprinted over to where he had stopped and begun twisting the gas cap off the square tank located under the seat.

"Be right back. Hold it up, will you?" he said and then turned and trotted back toward the barn.

John balanced the little, dusty two-wheeler, holding on to both of the worn grips protruding from the ends of the handlebars. A couple minutes later, Douglas came out with a red metal gas can in hand and a yellow funnel in the other.

He reached us and dropped the nose of the funnel in the minibike's tank, twisted the lid off the can, and began filling it up with gasoline. A little fuel overflowed, streaking the rusted tank, pooling on the top of the motor.

"We got a gusher here, boys!" Douglas exclaimed.

After placing the cap back on the tank and the lid on the gas can, he checked the oil by lightly turning a small, two-pronged metal knob lower down on the engine, pulling it straight out. Dark, thin oil dripped from the end of the indicator that was molded to the inner bottom of the cap.

"All systems are go."

He replaced the oil knob, reached over, flipped a toggle-switch upward, and then grasped a filthy handle and raised his head to the air and yelled at the top of his lungs, "Contact!"

A frayed, stained cotton rope emerged from inside the motor where it had lain coiled. He gave it a pull. The minibike sputtered.

Nothing.

Us boys wilted at the letdown. Douglas was undeterred.

"John, twist that handle all the way around when I pull the rope, okay?"

John nodded and Douglas again yelled, "Contact!" He gave it a mighty yank, and John manipulated the handle back toward himself. The exhaust pipe coughed a little longer than last time.

"Twist again. Go!"

Douglas gave it a superb pull, and the little bike sputtered to life.

"Woo-hoo! Yeah! Born to be wild!" Douglas screamed.

He reached over and took the controls from John, throttling the handle forward and back, keeping the motor going. Then he plopped down on the torn and tattered seat.

"I'm going to check it out, boys," he said. Then away he went, cutting through the backyard with light-blue smoke belching out the ass end of the bike, making big circles about three times before coming back. He seemed to be having one hell of a time while doing it. Arthur stepped out the back door and started shouting in his direction to "cut the crap" and then retreated inside.

"You guys ever ride bicycles?" he asked when he returned.

We had, but even if we hadn't, we damn sure would have convinced him we were experts at it. But Douglas wasn't taking any chances. He pulled John forward and walked him through the motions.

"It's just like that. Twist the handle for gas and push that square pedal by your left foot to use the brakes. You know right from left, right? Right?" he teased.

"You bet I do," our brother boasted, not getting the joke.

He had John climb aboard.

"Stay off the grass, look both ways when you get to the road, and then go to the corner and back. Now take off, Lone Ranger."

John sped off, a little shaky at first, but then he straightened up and Douglas bellowed, "Hi Ho Silver, away!"

John turned right and disappeared from our sight, the view blocked by the house. The three of us ran down the drive to the entrance and there he was, hauling ass up the road on that little, lawnmower-motor-driven minibike.

When he reached the corner at the top of the hill, he made a wide, looping turn and gunned the motor back toward us. When he got back to where we were waiting on him, he had a smile on his face ten-feet wide.

"Who's next?" Douglas asked.

Jason swung his leg up and over the seat and took off almost full-bore right from the get-go. He was back in no time, and it was my turn. I hopped on, goosed the gas, and took off in a state of complete exhilaration, a cool wind blowing through my hair. I reached the corner and emulated what my brothers had done and made my way back, feathering the brake pedal until I came to a complete stop, never wanting it to end.

"Good job, guys, but I can't let you ride it anymore," Douglas said.

He reached down, flipped the toggle to the off position, and killed the engine. The smiles that had been plastered across our faced disappeared just like that and our heads dropped.

Great, he's just like them, I thought.

He'd dangled the carrot on a string in our faces, and we had chased it. Now it was gone and here we were, as usual, left hungry.

"Hey, look at me," he said in a low, calm voice. "I, one hundred percent, cannot let you ride this beast..."

A big goofy smile broke over his face.

"Until you name it," he whispered.

We stared at him, and he started laughing uncontrollably.

"Well? What are you going to call it?"

"Rocket," I said.

Then came more suggestions from Jason and me.

"Black Stallion."

"Black Beauty."

"Speedy."

"Road Runner."

"Milton!"

That last one got a good laugh. I had suggested it because I had seen Milton Berle on television and thought he was funny, so why not?

John finally piped up and said, "How about Chugs."

Douglas looked at John and asked him, "Why Chugs?"

"Well, when you drive it down the road, it just chugs along."

Douglas started laughing. "Chugs sounds good to me. Let's put it to a vote."

No sooner had the word 'vote' passed his lips than all three of our hands flew up in the air and, I'll tell you what, at that moment it felt like we could have touched the clouds we had been observing not an hour ago.

"Well, it looks like it's unanimous," Douglas said. "Let's shake on it."

We all shook hands to seal the deal. Each shake of the hand from Douglas was exaggerated, pulling us forward and back.

"Now you don't have to ask for rides anymore."

A gentle smile crept across his face.

He walked off toward the house and we took turns riding that little motorized slice of heaven right until Douglas came back out with a care package stowed under his arm, preparing to leave and head on back to school. He tossed the brown paper bag through the open window of his faded Mercury and then opened the door and slid behind the wheel.

"I'll be back soon. Nice to meet you. Hold down the fort," he said with a grin.

He fired the engine up, radio still rocking that Kiss eight-track tape. He gave us a wave and backed out the drive and, as he put the old beater in drive, he hollered, "See you later, alligators!"

He sped off in a tremendous cloud of dust, us yelling back to him, "After a while, crocodile!"

And there went our friend down the road, leaving us behind for greener pastures. The two days he had been there, neither John nor Jason had wet the bed and I seemed to have been able to stomach whatever was put before me, which meant no beatings and no berating.

I wonder if it was because of him.

I'd like to believe it was.

CHAPTER EIGHTEEN

T he morning after Douglas left, I woke up to the familiar sounds of the basement coming alive with pain and anguish. They were distant and alien at first. Those few days with Douglas in the house made them seem like faulty memories, rewired for a while. But Walter's shouts were unmistakable, even through the floor that separated Robbie's bedroom from the basement below.

Someone had wet the bed.

Our break was over.

I found out later both John and Jason had wet the bed, so both barrels of Walter's rage were firing off bright and early instead of at night as they had been as of late. Walter almost seemed happy about the development when he stomped up the stairs. A smug, ugly grimace adorned that pudgy face of his. Or maybe it expressed delight. He reeked of satisfaction.

It wasn't the only thing that reeked that morning. I had a nice half-cup of unfinished, sour milk awaiting my consumption under the watchful eye of Carol for breakfast. I choked down and kept that unforgivable sin of food in my stomach and rushed outside. There was no Douglas there to break up the reforming routine of normal fear and anger.

The mattresses my brothers had soaked overnight lay draped

against each side of the weeping willow tree in the backyard, on full display from the road for any passing vehicles to gawk at. I wondered if they just thought we were airing them out. Could they see the stains from that far away? The three of us brothers met up, already tired of the return to routine and needing our escape, running to the barn for Chugs. As we pushed it through the barn door and made our way to the driveway, excited to get on and get going, Robbie came out and went to retrieve his motorcycle. He started it in the barn and rode through the door and over to where we were situated, just getting ready to pull the rope on our mighty steed. He killed the motor on his bike.

"That piece of shit used to be mine, but I outgrew it."

We didn't respond. Jason was pulling the rope on Chugs with no luck.

"You forgot to push the switch up," Robbie said.

"Thanks," Jason said, embarrassed that he'd already forgotten the step-by-step process.

"That thing is so slow compared to mine," Robbie continued. "I'll bet if I gave you a head start to the corner I could catch up to you and beat you back to the house."

"Probably," John said.

"No way," Jason protested, defending our new ride with great fervor.

"You want to bet?" Robbie said, was straddling his nicer, newer ride. "Never mind, you guys ain't got nothing to bet."

Well, he definitely got that right.

"You're on," Jason said, now staring at Robbie, determined to prove him wrong. "We have nothing to bet, but I know I can beat you back here as long as you promise not to take off until I get to the corner."

Robbie smiled, thrilled that Jason had taken the bait.

"Deal," he said.

Rules established, the two boys lined up in the middle of the dirt road that led to the half-way point.

"You promise not to leave early?" Jason asked one more time.

"I said I wouldn't, God, chuh," Robbie replied, shaking his head.

Jason throttled Chugs up and sped off toward the mile section, looking back once or twice to make sure Robbie kept his word. Robbie was laughing as Jason neared the corner and began revving his motor. When Jason reached the top of the hill and had begun his looping turn to race back to where we stood, Robbie tore—and I mean tore—out like a bat out of hell, making quick work getting to the corner.

"He's going to catch him," John determined.

It sure looked like it. Before Jason had even made it down the small incline to where the road flattened out, Robbie was pulling up on him. And then, the unthinkable happened in our favor. As Robbie went to make his turn, he overzealously gunned his motorcycle and, when he was almost turned back toward us, he laid his bike over hard.

Jason, at full throttle, and Chugs farting out a steady stream of blue smoke, were getting closer. Robbie frantically picked up his bike and began kicking that pedal as fast as he could. By the time he got it started and was roaring back in our direction, Jason was twenty yards from us. John and I started shouting.

"You can do it!"

"Come on, Chugs! Show him what we've got!"

Jason arrived well ahead of Robbie, greeted by our cheers. Jason came to a stop and John killed the motor. Robbie pulled up.

"That doesn't count. Do over. I get a do over!"

Jason was pushing Chugs from the road to the driveway and we were congratulating him all the way. John looked back at Robbie.

"It counts. He won."

Robbie rode over to the side of the house, jumped off his motorcycle, allowing it to crash to the ground. He jogged up in front of where Jason was and grabbed Chugs's handlebars, straddling the bald front tire, blocking him from advancing further.

"I said I get a do over," he repeated, his face trembling.

"But I won, Robbie, fair and square," Jason said.

"No, you didn't. You cheated."

Back and forth, they continued.

"I didn't cheat."

"Yes, you did."

"No, I didn't."

That's when Robbie made a huge mistake. He shoved Jason down and Chugs fell over on him. No sooner had the bike come to rest than—smack!—John had interceded, popping Robbie dead center of his mug. His legs gave out, and he went down like a sack of potatoes. John strad-dled him and pinned his arms over his head, secure against the ground. A small trickle of blood oozed from Robbie's nose as John leaned in real close to his face.

"If you ever touch one of my brothers again, you'll wish you were never born."

I had a few seconds to revel in my brother's righteous anger, preening at his badass takedown and threat. But it ended way too soon for us, ripped away before we could really enjoy it.

"Hey! You get your ass off him, you little bastard!"

What we didn't know at the time but figured out pretty fast was that Walter had been observing this brief altercation from the back corner of the house. I'm sure he'd been enjoying the moment his younger brother toppled Jason and Chugs. But when John cracked Robbie a good one and mounted him, rendering Robbie helpless, it was time to step in and, in Walter's eyes, even the score. He barreled toward us kind of fast, what with all that blubber he hefted around. Walter pulled John off Robbie and threw him backward across the grass and helped Robbie to his feet. Robbie, now sniffling and wiping the blood from his upper lip with the back of his arm, began telling his version of the truth.

"They cheated. They're cheaters and he punched me." He pointed at John.

Our older brother scrambled to his feet and stood in front of Jason, who had wriggled out from under Chugs.

"You're a real badass, you little sucker-punching pussy," Walter hissed.

"But he shoved Jason down first and Chu–"

"Shut up!" he shouted, cutting John off. "So you think you're real tough, don't you? Let's see how tough you are, badass."

John stood silent, not uttering a word.

"Get over here and lay down," Walter directed.

We were all silent, waiting. John didn't move. Then Walter screamed. "Now, pissant!"

John walked over to where Walter stood. Walter shoved him to the ground with one beefy hand.

"Flat on your back, boy," he sneered.

He began removing his belt. We knew what was coming next. Once the belt came off, he put it to use every time. Only this time, Walter put a twist on the "lesson" he'd be teaching John.

"You two get over here," he said, pointing to Jason and me. We scurried over to where Walter and Robbie stood and where John was lying at Walter's feet on his back, looking up. Walter folded his belt and snapped it together twice.

"Okay, pussy, you want to prove you can protect your brothers?"

A sinking feeling kicked off in my stomach.

"Well, now's your chance, badass... Robbie, get on top of him."

Robbie stood there and kind of just stared down at John and then back at Walter.

"Go ahead, sit on his chest." Walter pointed down at John.

"You better not hit me again," Robbie told John and straddled him with legs on either side of his torso. Then he looked at Walter for further instructions.

"Now, you little bastard, he's going to punch you right in the face and if you fight back or try to stop him, your brothers are going to get their asses beat, you understand?"

He popped the belt together a couple more times and then let it dangle down at his side.

"Do you understand!" he hollered.

John nodded he did.

Walter smiled. "Stretch your arms out."

John pulled his arms out from under Robbie's legs and placed them all the way out, horizontal to the earth. Looking down at him, lying underneath our youngest foster brother, he looked as though they'd nailed him to an invisible cross, right down to the blood on his shirt. Droplets from Robbie's nose.

"Punch him, Robbie, right now."

John turned his head to the side and looked at Jason and me. Fear-filled eyes went dead in an instant. We were peering into the eyes of a stranger. A moment later, he turned his head back in the forward position just as the first punch landed squarely on his left cheek. His head bounced up and back again, still facing forward.

"Again, Robbie," Walter ordered.

Now, raring back a little more than the first time and with a touch more enthusiasm, Robbie threw a haymaker to the same cheek, and it landed on the side of his mouth. John's head snapped to the right and again returned to where it started.

A small trickle of blood slipped from the corner of his mouth. Now, with no prompting, Robbie threw a left, a left, another right, taking time to line up each shot. John's face was turning pink and, with every blow that sent his head in our direction, our eyes met. He had a look on his face that said, *Don't worry, guys. I got this. He will not get to use that belt.* Another punch was a right jab to his left eye. It immediately began puffing up.

"That's enough, Robbie," Walter instructed, curtailing the lesson.

His last punch slowed and swatted the ground next to our older brother, just missing its mark. If Walter gave you an order, you listened, whether it was three little pieces of shit like us or blood relation. Robbie popped up, smiling at me and Jason, basking in his victory over the much tougher competitor who lay before him, bruised and bleeding.

"Take off, Robbie," Walter said.

Robbie went to his motorcycle and picked it up off the ground, his unearned victory already forgotten. John rolled over onto his knees. Walter walked over to John and kicked him square in the ass, sending him sprawling forward and gasping for air.

"Real tough guy, aren't you?"

John said nothing.

"Aren't you!"

Walter swung the belt around in a high arc and it came blistering down across John's back with a loud crack.

That, we assumed, was his closing curtain call. Satisfied with his performance, he threaded the belt back around his overlapping waist. Then, he quickly waddled toward his pickup, parked in its usual spot. He ripped the driver's side open and leaned in, scrambling for something. He hefted himself back out and onto his feet and headed our way, birthing hips weeble-wobbling back and forth. In his right hand, gripped tight, was a pair of pliers.

Now what? Is he going to pull a few of John's teeth for good measure?

He bypassed all three of us and made his way to the minibike, our minibike, jerking it up on its tires and kicking the stand down. The big bastard plopped down on his fat ass, removed a wire and twisted the top of the sparkplug with the pliers. When it was loose, he jammed the grips into his back pocket and began unscrewing one of the essential pieces needed to bring Chugs to life. The oily plug appeared in his right hand. He struggled to his feet with an audible grunt and walked toward the road in front of the house. Leaning back, and with all his might, he chucked the sparkplug over the road and across the fence. The precious part disappeared into a sea of grass that had overtaken the property owned by some other family. In all his ungraceful glory, he made his way back to Chugs, all red-faced and sweaty, kicking it over much the way he had our brother.

"Good luck winning any fucking races when you're pushing it down the road, you little bastards."

He turned toward John. "And don't you ever lay a hand on any family member of mine again, you piece of shit."

He walked back to his truck, threw the pliers onto the bench seat, slammed the door, and huffed off toward the back of the house.

Meanwhile, John was getting to his feet and stumbling toward the road. He collapsed to his knees in the deep ditch that ran in front of our personal prison. Dropping his head to his chest, he let his arms dangle at his sides.

"Hey, John?" Jason squeaked out. "Are you—?"

"Leave me alone." His chest was heaving with each gulp of air.

The tone he used was persuasive enough to shut him up. Jason looked at me. "Let's get Chugs back to the barn."

I nodded and helped Jason lift the now useless hunk of metal and rubber back upright, positioning myself behind it while Jason took the handles. We pushed the minibike back to its weather-beaten wooden coffin.

Not one of us ever felt that moment of freedom again. Sure, after a while when things had cooled down, I asked as nice as possible, on what I thought was a good day, but the answer from Walter was always, "Nope, cheaters never prosper."

John showed no interest in wanting to get Chugs back to life. John never took much interest in anything again while we were there, including Jason or me. When he took another one for the team, it robbed something from him he never got back. If there was a sliver of compassion in his body, he didn't show it.

Compassion.

CHAPTER NINETEEN

T here's a chair in the corner. Pull it over in front of him. Talk all you want, just no contact, understand?"

I nod. John's head had raised as Sheriff Luxemburg opened the door to the interrogation room. He sits staring right at me. His expression is blank, as though he is looking through me. He raises one hand and shoots the bird in my direction.

"Hello to you, too, John," I say.

"Nah, bro, not intended for you. Pass it on beside you to your new fucking pig friend."

Sheriff Luxemburg just shakes his head, a little smile forming on his lips. "Good luck," he says. He takes two steps back as I step through. The door closes behind me. A metallic thunk proves that it is now locked.

It is official.

Luxemberg has shut me in with a monster that, only hours before, had murdered a man in cold blood. I grab my seat and drag it across the floor. Its legs screech, abrasive. Nails on a chalkboard.

"Pick it up, man, goddamn. You've always been able to annoy me within two seconds of seeing you."

I lift the chair and place it just out of arm's reach, in case he feels the need to put me "through a fucking wall", one of his favorite sayings. He sits on a metal bench that is bolted to the wall, still in his civilian clothes, camouflaged with blood.

"Guess they don't have the customary orange jumpsuits here, do they?"

He smiles. "Oh, they have them. I didn't feel like wearing one."

"You did what you did and gave up, John. It's over. Why fight them?"

The smile disappears from his face. "I'm not done yet," he says.

A chill runs the length of my spine and I shift in my chair, my balls still aching courtesy of Deputy Dickhead.

"I'd say this brief trip down memory lane has run its course, John."

He looks away, focused on the corner of the cell, lost in time.

I need him to speak, to explain himself. To recite his side of this incredible mess.

"You committed murder. You killed a man."

"I killed the DEVIL!" he erupts.

I want to see insanity in his eyes, but they look familiar. Too familiar. That aged and jaded face. Then he calms himself.

"You don't know what it was like in that basement, man."

"I was down there, too, John. Don't act like you were the only one who went through that shit, brother."

He scoffs. "You were down in that basement for what, two, maybe three months? We were down there the entire time. Do you have any idea what it's like to sleep with the goddamn devil on the other side of the wall for over a year?"

"Don't give me that shit, John. I was getting mine upstairs almost as much as you two. It's not my fault I didn't wet the goddamn bed."

I'm fuming now, remembering back on the times I was bent over that dining-room table. Staring at that fucking clock. Getting shellacked for something as simple as a spoonful of cream of wheat left in the bowl's bottom.

"It's not the same," he says. "How many times was a boot to the head your wake-up call, Joseph?"

"Never," I say.

"How many times were you stripped bare and made to whip your brother? And if I didn't do it hard enough, that fat son of a bitch would take up the belt and beat our naked asses until we bled or passed out? How many times, Joseph?"

Oh... naked... that... that's new.

John never talked about details when it came to the basement. Lord knew I'd never gotten Jason to say anything about it, not that we wanted to. I slump back for a minute. The things that had happened to us, and to my brothers down in that basement, were inexcusable. I had never found it in myself to forgive a single one of them for what they had done to us.

But I had never found it in me to put a slug in any of them, either.

"That doesn't justify murder, John."

My answer feels wrong the second it passes through my teeth. A bad feeling worms its way into my gut.

A tear forms in the corner of one eye, pooling on the lower lid until it spills quickly down one cheek. He wipes away what he considers weakness with a quick backhand, followed by a swipe to the leg, allowing it to soak into the fibers of his jeans.

"Do you know what really happened that morning?"

I rest my chin on my chest and fold my hands together in my lap, wringing them.

I don't.

It is my greatest relief and my biggest regret. It always has been.

"Do you have any idea what it's like to watch your little brother curl up, hands clenched tight and pulled to his chest, writhing in pain, half-naked on a filthy cement floor?"

Yes.

"Do you have any idea what it's like to watch him fight until he can't fight anymore?"

I remember.

His voice is monotone. He's narrated this to himself before, over and over, until the words had lost their meaning.

My eyes fill.

"Do you know what a snoring last breath sounds like coming from a nine-year-old boy who's had enough? Do you?"

No.

"No, you don't. You know what it's like to not finish breakfast and get a spanking for it. Bravo, bro, bravo." He says this with a few slow claps.

"That's not fair, John."

"Life's not fair, Joseph, get used to it."

We fall into silence. John has said his piece. He isn't itching to fill the ringing quiet with any small talk. I can't think of anything to say to make the pulsing blood in my ears settle down.

"So here you are, John," I finally say.

"Yeah, here I am."

"There's no amount of money and no amount of lawyers gonna be able to pull the rabbit from the hat on this one, buddy. You're fucked."

He sits there on the cold metal and just smiles. Smiles. What the fuck was running through his mind right before he lost it?

"You know what, man, I understand why you did what you did but–"

He cuts me off quick. "Do you? Do you understand? I don't think you do, Joseph."

"Well, enlighten me, man!"

My raised voice aggravates him. You can see on his face.

He leans forward, champing at the bit to drag me down, kicking and screaming into the nightmare he had been living since we were kids.

He hisses, "Calm down and listen, buddy. I'm only telling this story once, so listen up and listen good, got it?"

"Oh, you're gonna have to tell this story again and again, John, you can take that to the bank."

He looks amused.

"Once," he says.

CHAPTER TWENTY

After Walter introduced his "no-fight-back" policy, they kept John from attending school for three days until the swelling around his eye had subsided and the bluish-purple bruising around the socket had turned a nasty shade of yellow. He arrived back in class on a Friday, a day before spring break was to begin. He hadn't really made friends, so it seems nobody bothered to ask, including school staff.

Odd why somebody didn't say something. There had to have been occasions where either of my brothers' appearances or their withdrawn and skittish personalities had to have thrown up a red flag. But then, it was a different time. Perhaps whatever happened at home was nobody's business, so as not to stir a pot that wasn't burning on your stove.

So, that Friday and the weekend following it came and went without incident, with no one paying any mind to John's long absence or fading bruises. There was no daring rescue to bring us from the unrelenting grip of the family. Despite that, the bastards seemed wary of how far they had gone and cooled down, except for a few verbal jabs here and there to keep us honest.

"Your mom is a crazy whore."

"Your dad is a lazy drunk."

No matter how many times we heard them refer to our parents in such a derogatory manner, it hurt.

The first day of our spring break started with the usual chores expected of us. We kicked hay, we cleaned, they screamed and administered small doses of discipline.

Then it was off to the lumberyard in Ridgeway to lend a hand with whatever needed done. But when we arrived, we had our first break from routine. Carol called us to the front desk by the cash register and produced three nickels, one for each of us.

"Here you go, kiddos, get you some candy from the machine," she said.

Her eyes weren't as kind as her words. It made her voice sound false and brown sugar sweet. Hearing it was like needing a drink to wash down the last bite of dark chocolate cake that sits like a log in your throat.

In complete shock, we accepted the coins, one at a time, and made our way to the handful of treats that awaited us. We each took a turn, sliding a five-cent piece into the slot made just for that denomination, manipulating the handle clockwise.

After a full revolution of the silver toggle, around six or seven candy-coated pieces of chocolate tumbled into the palms of our palms. I almost expected the treat to be slapped right out of my hands before I could feel the weight of them in my palm. But nothing like that happened, and the confections stayed right there, a mouthwatering weight in my hands.

Holy smokes, a treat? Of our very own?

We didn't know why and, to be honest, we didn't care why. This was the first bit of sweets we had gotten since the Sullivan's farm and *hallelujah*. It was fantastic.

Each of us boys let the sweet treats slowly melt in our mouths, one by one, until they dissolved right down to nonexistence. While finishing our reward, we made our way to the back, where we would wait for any directives that may come our way, like helping load lumber or sweeping up in the saw room. The act of kindness from this abrasive, noxious woman had stunned Jason and me.

John didn't seem to give a shit.

He hadn't given a shit about too awful much after the recent pummeling he'd received.

Feeling energized from the shot of sugar we'd ingested, Jason and I began running circles around sawhorses in an impromptu game of tag. A familiar face came around the corner and peered inside the saw room.

Virginia was smiling at us when we noticed her, and the questions began.

"Are you here to pick us up?"

"Are we leaving?"

"Are we going home?"

She waited until we settled down and then gathered us near her.

"I'm here to ask you boys some questions," she said, still smiling. She lined us up on a stack of lumber, staged for future use, and asked, "How's it going? Are you guys doing okay?"

We stared at her. That was a loaded question, if ever there was one. What were we supposed to say? Was this what the candy had been for? A bribe? Was Carol standing just outside the door, listening in?

But if that was the case, John was past giving a shit.

"No, we are not doing okay," he blurted out.

Virginia frowned and looked at him and asked him to elaborate.

John told her about the flyswatter and the crazy counting. "And if one of us wets the bed, Walter whips us bad, and he shot us with a gun. Sometimes Arthur wakes me up by throwing a boot at my head in the morning. Joseph has to drink sour milk after school. They let Robbie beat me up and they call Mom and Dad terrible names."

Virginia sat on the cut boards, not saying a word, just shaking her head up and down while John spilled his guts.

Jason and I interjected with "yeah, yeah, yeah," with each confession from our older brother's mouth.

John's voice carried like he wanted to keep going, but he ran out of breath and steam the longer Virginia stayed quiet. He trailed off. We waited.

"Okay, okay, boys, let's all calm down. I'm sure it's not that bad. They shot you? Come on, fellas."

"It's true, Virginia," we all said, nodding our heads and pleading our cases.

"Jason passed out once," John said in a desperate voice.

I begged, "Can we go home to Mom and Dad? Please, Virginia, please."

"Well," she said, "Your mom still isn't well enough to take care of you the way she needs to." She mentioned nothing about our dad.

"Until she's better, you'll have to stay here."

The air felt as though it had just left the saw room. What energy the small amount of sugar had provided exited right along with any hope of escaping. She promised it wouldn't be much longer, and we'd be going home because our mom was making strides every day. Just as soon as she was all better, we'd be back together.

"I have to go up front and talk to Carol and I'll be right back, okay?"

She had us stay seated. After about half an hour, she returned and began saying her goodbyes.

"I'll be back soon to check on you guys," she said.

She gave each of us a hug and walked around the corner of the building, leaving us there in the shaded saw room.

I can't remember if she was hesitant to leave us where we were, or dismissive of what she thought were tall tales. I can't recall now if she was angry or just a blank wall, unresponsive to our pleas.

We just remember that the person we counted on to save us, to take us away from pain and suffering and put us somewhere safe and happy, had failed to be the savior we thought she could be.

Just a short while after she exited, Frank came to the back and gave us instructions about an order that needed filled and we began searching for proper sizes of lumber that would need to be cut down to proper length. We spent the day doing this and other menial jobs until it was time to close up shop. The three of us were quiet while we worked. Our hopes raised and dashed again. It was like when Douglas left, only worse. We didn't have the energy for much else after.

Carol loaded us up in the family wagon and we drove back to the house. We pulled up and began unloading when she instructed us to come in and sit on the living room floor. She walked to the dining room and disappeared into the kitchen. We could hear her descending the basement stairs.

Dead silence.

"We're in trouble," John said.

Give that man a cigar!

When she returned, Walter was following close behind her, twisting his belt in both hands. She positioned herself smack dab in front of us and began.

"She hits me with a flyswatter."

Oh shit.

"Walter whips us for wetting the bed. Walter shoots us with a gun." Her sickly-sweet lilt was imitating a child's whiny voice.

Either she had listened in on our private conversation with the social worker or Virginia had told her everything we'd confided in her. I hoped, for the sake of memory, Virginia was a good person. Surely she hadn't ratted us out.

Either way, Carol had found out what John said, and she was angry. We were in for it now.

"Jason passed out and Joseph drinks soured milk!" she screamed. Her voice was shrill and indignant, as if we were spreading lies about her. One almost had to be impressed at her ability to muster up such outrage and sincerity.

I remember looking up at them, pure terror washing over my entire body. She was a monster from a late night show we had seen at home on a program called *Dimension Sixteen*. Her disgusting, failing teeth lay bare. Her faced seemed to contort with each outburst. Walter remained behind her, twisting that goddamn belt between his doughy hands, looking like a fat, coiled truck spring just waiting to unwind, releasing its energy all over our asses.

In an instant, her face softened and her thin lips came together and occluded those stained chompers, spittle collecting at the edges of her mouth.

"Walter," she began in a saccharin sweet voice, still looking down at the three of us now cowering on the carpeted floor. "Punish these liars, son."

All hell broke loose.

He lit into us worse than any other time up to that point. He beat our asses with that belt on every inch of our bodies except our face. When one of us would wiggle or squirm off in a direction he hadn't specified, he'd put his boot under our belly or hips and lift us back on the begging, pleading, and screaming pile of adolescence that was us.

I'm not sure how long this went on because I don't remember blacking out. John said it lasted quite a while. All I know is that it lasted. It ground on long enough for me to pass out. The last thing I remember was Jason's fading screams. When I came to, it was ending and Carol was getting her point across, loud and clear.

"And if you *ever* tell lies about us again, you'll wish you'd never been born!" she exclaimed. She looked like she had somehow been in on the beatings as well. Her hair hung loose, obscuring her haggard face. Splotched skin bore red mottling, like a bad sunburn.

Walter had left the room and Jason was a crumpled, bawling mess lying next to me. John was halfway back up on his ass. He had not shed a single tear. He just laid there, staring up at her as she finished what she had to say. I don't think a person can ever get used to that kind of abuse happening to them. In my oldest brother's case, I believe he just somehow managed to not give them the satisfaction they were after.

Have you ever seen the shirt, or a printed picture of an enormous owl swooping, descending upon a small mouse which, in preparing to be devoured, gives that nasty old owl the middle finger?

Written under the image is the phrase:

"The Last Great Act of Defiance."

John was like that goddamn mouse.

CHAPTER TWENTY-ONE

W e spent the rest of our spring break at the lumberyard. Going back to school was like being pardoned from the long days of picking through lumber and sorting it. I was happy to be back and picked up where I left off before the break, rough housing with the guys and chasing the girls. The well-balanced diet of school lunches beat stomaching bologna and mustard every day, that was for sure.

I filled the handful of remaining school weeks studying while in class to ensure the satisfactory marks I'd achieved held in place. Improving in subjects like arithmetic, which had given me fits for most of the school year, occupied most of my time.

The weeks melted away and, before I knew it, I was saying goodbyes to my new friends. Many of my peers brought talk of summer plans to the table. Trips to amusement parks and vacations permeated the air. I was envious, of course, assuming my summer would instead hold long, monotonous days at one of two lumberyards. There was that word again, though.

Assume.

My assumption proved correct for the first three weeks of summer. Temperatures rose. Days grew unbearable as we scrambled around, trying to keep up with orders presented to us that needed sorted and loaded.

One morning, that all changed.

It was close to the end of June when we got our first lesson in the art of hauling hay. Instead of grinding it out at the lumberyard, we hopped into the bed of the truck and snaked our way deep into the fields. They presented each of us with a steel hook adorned with a black, rubber-encased handle.

Simply put, it looked just like it sounds. It's what you'd find protruding from the cuff of the malevolent captain that chased Peter Pan or hanging from your car door, compliments of an urban legend.

Arthur drove us out to one of the family-owned pastures away from the farm, some miles down the road. We pulled through a barbed-wire gate and made our way to a large, red flatbed truck near the fence line. Attached to the side of the bed was a vertical, steel-caged, chain-driven tract. When lined up, even with a square bale, the machine would lift it up to the bed and spit it out.

Walter was waiting for us. He had us climb up and sit down on the wooden bed of the truck. Arthur slid into the cab, started it up, and began driving out into the pasture where hundreds of bales dotted the flat landscape.

"See all those bales of hay, boys?" he called up to us. "You're about to touch them all."

Standing up there with my hook in hand, I thought, *So we're working today, something different. It can't be any worse than the lumberyards.*

This turned out to be one of the most uneducated thoughts that had ever crossed my mind.

Arthur positioned the track in front of the first row of bales and hollered, "Ready?"

Walter instructed, "The bale is going to lift straight up the track and kick over. That's when two of you peckerheads will bury your hook in one end and drag it in place. I'll start the stack. Just do what I do and keep up, you got it?"

Still confused, we nodded in agreement. He yelled down to Arthur to take off. The first bale entered the caged opening on the ground and hooks attached to the chain embedded themselves in the bale. Up it came.

When it reached the top, it flipped over and Walter buried both hooks he had at the ends. With great ease, he placed it on the front passenger side of the wooden bed with a thump. Next up were John and Jason. The bale came up and flopped over and my brothers sunk a hook on each end and muscled it over to where Walter had deposited one, butting it up at the ends.

"Help me with the next bale, Joseph."

I thought to myself, *Don't screw up, don't screw up.*

The bale arrived and Walter swung his hook into the end before it hit the truck bed.

"Hurry!" he yelled.

I whipped my hook, and it slid effortlessly. Walter and I made our way to the line.

"You have got to lift. You can't just drag the thing, damn it."

My first attempt at this new chore and he was already on my ass.

After a while, and much like everything else in life, practice made perfect. We were stacking bales and keeping up. The cherry on top? Robbie was waiting at the fence, his motorcycle perched on its kickstand. Arthur came to a stop and Robbie took one of Walter's hooks and replaced him up top with the three of us. The spoiled little shit had to break a sweat, too.

Arthur took off and lined up another row and kept the same pace as before, Walter directing us on where to stack each bale.

Like anything that becomes familiar, we got quicker. The four of us figured out the faster we could stack, the more of a breather we got between turns. Or so we thought.

Walter yelled down to his dad, "Speed it up!"

Temperatures were rising right along with the speedometer. Perspiration increased from a trickle to a downpour. We held our own for a while. This was a task undertaken in the summer by teenage boys trying to get in shape for the upcoming football season. Not bad considering we were four young boys, the oldest ten, two aged nine, and one seven.

Each bale weighed between fifty and seventy pounds, dependent upon moisture content. Of course, I didn't know any of this while struggling to transport them. They may as well have gone for five hundred pounds each.

It wasn't long before we were wearing out. The morning dragged on. Hands slipped, chaffed, then blistered from the sweat and constant shifting of our grips. Our arms burned. Our lungs strained. After a while, my hands cramped. It was difficult to maintain a firm grip. My fingers barely had the strength to keep the hook properly positioned. But then, when it seemed we couldn't drag another bale, they stopped and gave us a water break.

The cells in my body were crying out for the clear liquid in every ladleful. It could have been pond water and I would have gulped it down, begging for more. Arthur and Walter allowed us time to cool down under the truck for a few minutes, but only a few. When it was time to get going again, Robbie bitched and Walter told him to shut up and get to work. He let a small "chuh" escape his lips, only to be met with his older brother mocking him.

"Chuh, chuh, chuh. Quit whining, you little baby."

The three of us would have been rolling on the ground laughing if we had the energy. We did laugh about it later when it was just the three of us alone. Walter, Robbie's personal bodyguard when John was getting the better of him, was now lumping him in with the likes of us. He had to work just as hard as they made us. The choice wasn't his to make. Neither was it ours, of course. The bales kept coming; we kept stacking. When it seemed not another bale could fit on the truck and we could not stack any higher, Walter finished the top of the stack all by his lonesome. It felt good to sit back and watch the fat bastard work while we did nothing, if only for a moment. It was over.

Walter slid off the back of the flatbed, making his way to the cab and got in. Arthur pulled the truck through the gate. We rode atop tight, packed bales down a dirt road, the summer air providing some relief, drying our sweat-soaked bodies, rumbling away from the pasture.

We arrived at a farm with a white barn in worse shape than the one behind our foster home. The structure looked like a strong wind could blow it over, reducing it to a pile of kindling at any moment. Another piece of farm machinery, also a vertical lift with hooks on a chain-driven track, was present.

The end was level with the truck bed. It rose from the ground at a forty-five-degree angle, jagged hooks running its length. The opposite end poked through an opening on the second story of the building, right up near the roof.

It didn't take a rocket scientist to figure out we would deposit the stacked bales of hay on the lift. They'd climb their way up to the opening and they wouldn't be jumping off the machine by themselves.

Nope. Our work had just reached the halfway point, and our day had just gotten longer.

Lunch was to be consumed first, and I was looking forward to it. I was famished and could use the nourishment. My legs were shaky, my head swooned with hunger. On the other side of the truck, next to the old barn, was a quaint, white, two-story farmhouse with faded green shutters.

Inside were two tables pushed together and draped with blue-and-white checkered tablecloths. A large bowl of fried chicken caught my eye first, followed by a couple bags of potato chips and two large, glass pitchers filled with ice, overflowing with brewed tea. Carol was setting plates out neatly in rows. My eyes must have been as large as picture windows as I took it all in.

Waiting at the very end of the table were three blue Tupperware cups and a plate with six scrumptious bologna and mustard sandwiches and a bag of plain chips. They would not be inviting us to dine with family that afternoon.

Why? Why did they pull this shit? We'd pulled our weight as much as the others all morning long. It wasn't fair. It was the little things like this that would eat you up inside. While they gulped their iced tea and tore meat from bone, we sat at the end designated for second-class citizens. We drank warm water from the cooler that had been side-mounted to the truck, eating our sandwiches, filthy fingerprints from our overworked hands embedded in the white bread.

After pounding down two sandwiches each, we followed Walter into the barn, up a rickety wooden ladder to the loft. It was here the bales from the truck would, after making their way up the track, find their new home. Arthur, Robbie, and Frank, the latter having finally made his appearance, began depositing bales, one-by-one, from the truck onto the lift.

It was on.

The difference between putting them on the truck and laying them up for storage was night and day. Our speed had to double just to stay even. The guys on the truck were allowing little to no space between each bale. The pace was furious, and so was Walter.

"Hurry!"

"Faster!"

"Move, damn it!"

Putting up the bales that quick was nice because, before we knew it, the truck bed was empty, littered with loose strands of hay. The not-so-enjoyable part was that they completely wore us out. It was hot up in the loft, with no breeze except that bastard's breath from yelling at us the entire time.

After making our way down the old ladder and drinking as much water as we could take in, we loaded up on the truck and headed back. Not to the house, but to the pasture. Already exhausted as we pulled up to the first row, we listened to Arthur yell, "Ready?"

Without waiting for a response, he put the truck in gear and so began round two. We got one-third of the way through a full load before Jason and I missed a bale. It fell to the edge of the bed and off onto the ground. The truck came to a stop.

"Who missed that bale?" Arthur demanded.

Jason told him it was us and that we couldn't get to it fast enough. Arthur called us down and, whipping our asses with his belt, explained the importance of never letting one hit the ground.

"We have to stop and place it in front of the lift or circle around and pick it up," he said. "That burns fuel and time, idiots, now get up there and move your asses. You better not miss another." He didn't seem to realize the irony of wasting time and energy beating the shit out of us, of course.

The whipping, Arthur must have thought, was proper motivation. I guess it served its purpose. It had my brother and me hopping, ignoring the pain in our cramped hands and legs, though our butts and legs burned for the rest of the afternoon. He could have explained to us a better way to stack or grab the payload that might have been more efficient. But, this was not the way this family got their point across.

We managed, with no more stops, to fill the truck and head to the barn again. Once there, we had more water and then it was back to the loft for more stacking. John remained on the truck this time and Robbie joined Jason and me up top. The bales began making their way up and we were off to the races again.

Halfway through the load, John, who had not been letting up and had been feeding them to us as fast as the others, lost his footing, slipping on loose remnants of hay that coated the slick, wooden truck bed, falling on the conveyor.

As luck would have it, he landed on the open steel frame and moving chain and just–by the narrowest of margins–missed the hooks that ran along the monstrosity. Arthur hustled to stop the drive motor after John had sped along half the length of the lift.

"Get down here!" he yelled.

John rolled over and began crawling down on his hands and knees, doing his best balancing act. When he reached arm's length, Arthur grabbed him by the hair, jerked him hard to the ground, and began kicking John with the heel of his right boot.

"Don't you ever scare me like that again, you bastard!"

The barrage of blows continued as we looked down from the second floor, helpless to do anything–not that we could. It had become commonplace, and it was becoming an all too familiar way of life. As John writhed in pain on the ground, receiving blow after blow, I couldn't help but wonder if they ever considered the fear he must have felt when he lost his footing or when he fell toward his possible impalement on large steel hooks.

Did they ever consider the fear we felt when we thought our brother, dumped at our feet, pierced and bleeding, would be much worse?

I can say, with great certainty, that our feelings, whether scared or hurting, were the furthest thing from those people's minds.

After John dragged himself to his feet, he climbed back up onto the truck bed–worse for wear but not giving them the satisfaction–and completed the rest of the work alongside Frank.

Then we were back on the truck bed, watching the road and dreading our next run. Would my legs have the strength? Would my stomach be able to hold down the sandwiches I had scarfed down? What if I was the next to fall onto the conveyor belt? Would I be as lucky as John if I fell, or would I experience what those inanimate hay bales did when the hooks sank deep into them?

When we realized the truck was not returning to the pasture and was instead making its way home, we collapsed. I felt heavy and light at the same time. My arms throbbed against the numbness that had set in halfway through. Robbie might have moaned complaints at some point, but if he did, I did not tune my ears to the little prick's complaints.

The next day started the entire process over. My body fought against an ache that it hadn't gotten used to, even with the frequent beatings and lumber hauling from the past few months. I might have cried at some point. It may have just been sweat pouring down into my eyes.

When I try to remember the third day, I just recall a feeling of overwhelming numbness. Perhaps I had zoned out and let my body do the work while my mind retreated away from the pain and exhaustion. I can't quite recall what happened on that third day, but I remember that when the final bale got put up, there wasn't a single "good job".

Not even a "thank you".

I'd never worked so hard in my young life. Later, during my teenage years, local farmers would put out the word that there was money to be had in the fields. My peers jumped at the opportunity. I never gave it a second thought.

CHAPTER TWENTY-TWO

S ummer was in full swing by the time we finished hauling hay. Our days went back to being predictable. My brothers managed not to ruin the sheets on the daily. Spoiled eats and boots to the head were ever present, per usual. But, when chores were complete, we'd plod up the road to the church and climb the colossal tree, the boneyard general, always on guard and in command of its stationary tombstone sentries.

When the feeling of elevated freedom bored us, we'd walk to the creek bed, just across the road, trying to find the biggest crawdads we could secure. After an intense inspection, we would release our catch back into the cool water and watch them dart off tail-first. Sometimes I wished we could be like those crawdads, slipping through the current and far away from the big humans that had turned their world into a runaway rollercoaster. What would it be like to leave the awful moments far behind you and just go back to living your life? It felt as though I'd never know again.

One sweltering afternoon, Carol put my brothers to work, pulling weeds in the garden on the north side of the house. It was a sweaty and tedious chore I very much disliked. God forbid you didn't clear them all out to her specifications.

"You missed some," she'd bark. "The weeds will suck the life right out of them beans if you don't rip them out by the roots."

We spent hours on our knees pulling them little green bastards, but it was never good enough.

"No water break until that garden is clean. They'll suck the life, they'll suck the life!" she'd bellow. If anyone was sponging the life out of anything regularly, it was her, not the small cadmium green interlopers.

While they did that, Arthur instructed Robbie to teach me how to run the lawnmower. It wasn't a new, gasoline-powered cutter. It was a walk-behind clipper. The dual set of blades on the orange, man-powered machine would spin as the wheels made revolutions. I was excited. This would be my first attempt at cutting grass, ever. Robbie gave me a quick tutorial and then I was off and mowing back and forth.

The fresh smell of grass permeated the air. I was glad to be moving around, a cool breeze chilling the tendrils of sweat that ran down my forehead and neck. My brothers were baking in the dirt with little air movement while I was creating my own.

"You missed a spot," Carol would holler, her bony index finger wagging to an uneven strip of grass I'd neglected.

Circling back, I'd take careful aim and the taller lengths would disappear, courtesy of Joseph. Yes, I was actually having fun. I finished the back and headed out front to complete the yard in its entirety.

"My turn," Robbie said. He grabbed the handles away from me and disappeared around the side of the house, mower blades whirring off in the distance.

It was a bummer, but at least I'd missed out on the sore fingers and knees that weeding caused. Walter arrived home and since, we hadn't fucked up, he ignored us and went inside. After John and Jason finished weeding, they left us to our own devices. We played tag and other games to pass the time until seasoned beans and cornbread called our names. The dinner bell rang, and we took our places at the end of the table and began sopping the brown lacquer in our bowls with the yellow, caked bread. We finished and deposited our bowls and cups in the sink and then tried to make the best of what sunlight remained. Just as it set, we became involved in a serious game of hide-and-seek.

Arthur hollered, "Joseph, get over here!"

I ran to the back stoop from the brush pile that had been my place of concealment.

"Did you finish cutting the grass?"

"Yes," I whispered.

Was he blind? Hadn't he seen the magnificent work I'd done?

"No, you didn't, boy," he said.

He began pointing to different spots in the yard I had missed or hadn't trimmed to his satisfaction. I stood there in silence, bummed out.

"Go! Get the mower and finish the job."

I ran toward the barn, wrestled the machine through the side door, and scurried back to the yard.

"Finish," he said. And then he turned and retreated through the door.

I began scanning the yard for any spots I may have missed and that's when the entire green landscape turned, right before my eyes, as flat and even as plate-glass. My eyes, frantic, darted around the yard, looking for imperfections. All the while, the sun was mocking me.

Having a hard time seeing, buddy?

Every second that evaporated stole the precious light I needed to complete my task. I ran back and forth as fast as I could, not knowing if I was hitting the marks he'd pointed out.

The terrain transformed, growing black because of the lack of natural light. The small amount of artificial illumination coming from the small kitchen window may as well have been a single match to light my way through Hades. Arthur returned right on time.

He won't be able to see if I hit every blade he wanted mowed over again. No way.

A beam of light broke the pitch where I stood and dread saturated me. He had a flashlight. Dammit.

He bounced down the stairs and conveyed his dissatisfaction.

"Nope, you're not done."

Well, I guess I'll finish it tomorrow, was what went through my mind.

He produced a pair of steel scissors and plopped them in one of my hands and the flashlight in the other.

"Hop to it," he said.

For the next hour, I belly-crawled, cutting blades of grass a couple at a time, not even knowing if I was in the right spot. Then he reemerged, took up the flashlight, and, after sweeping the darkened yard, hauled off and kicked me square in the ass. Pain shot all the way to the top of my head and my breath exited along with a quick cry. As he buried a size-twelve in my ass, the scissors flew from my hands and landed in front of me. I scrambled to retrieve them, all the while desperate for air.

"Next time I come out here, it better be right," he said and then walked away, dropping the flashlight back in my hands.

I gathered my senses and continued snaking my way through the grass, sweat pouring off me. I was scampering around in the dark close to midnight when he returned and deemed the job satisfactory. Still not knowing if I'd made a difference, I went in, ass bruised and aching, and took a hot bath. I climbed in bed and Robbie, still wide awake, said, "I didn't miss a single blade of grass up front." Little prick.

Even if you had, there's no way you'd be out there in the middle of the night with scissors and a flashlight, I thought to myself.

He turned his back to me and I flipped him the bird.

July was uneventful. However, we got to go to the high school baseball diamond and watch the Fourth of July fireworks display, so that was nice. A rare treat of one hotdog and a soda to boot. After the delicious, caramelized nectar disappeared, it was the water fountain for us boys—Robbie excluded, of course. It seemed he had unlimited funds for July Fourth food and drinks.

Summer continued with whippings every other day and toiling in the lumberyards. Saturdays, we went to church and Sundays... Well, Sundays were not a day of rest for us. It was work, work, work.

August rolled around and, to our surprise, while we were sweating it out at the other lumberyard, Virginia showed up. She wanted to talk to us again. She led us to the large storage facility across the alley where enormous lengths of wood collected dust. Just like before, she sat us on a stack of uncut lumber and began asking the same questions.

"How are you guys doing? Is everything okay?"

Unlike before, we sat in silence.

"Hey, we have privacy here, okay?" she said.

John opened up about the last time we told on them and got it something terrible. As he spilled his guts, Carol's head darted into the opening of the building, receding as fast as it had appeared.

She was listening! John caught her and immediately shut down.

"Go on, it's okay," Virginia encouraged.

"Everything's fine. We're good," he said.

After prying for a few more minutes, she called it good and turned to leave. "By the way, boys, you're going to see your mom and dad next weekend."

Holy shit, what? Did I hear that hear right, or was it a dream?

"Serious?" Jason asked.

"You bet I am, and they can't wait to see you boys. I'll see you next Saturday morning. Bye, boys." And with that, she walked away.

I was so happy. I was welling up with tears and Jason was chattering a hundred miles an hour.

"I can't believe it. This is great!"

Then John said what hadn't even crossed my mind.

"I'm telling Dad and he is going to kill them when he hears how they've treated us."

The building fell silent as we imagined what that would be like. Our large, ass-kicking father was going to give them what we had been getting, and I loved the thought. It seemed like a fair deal to me, and to my brothers as well. John jumped down and hustled to the large opening, peeking around the doorjamb, then looked back at us.

"Did you see her spying on us?"

Yes, all three of us had seen her.

Virginia had been situated with her back to the opening and was clueless Carol had been there, waiting like a spider in a darkened corner, ready to pounce when alerted by the slightest vibration of its sticky, silken threads.

Hope had been absent from us for some time, but with good—no, great—news just laid at our feet, we walked on air back to the office. Carol sat at the desk, a dour look on her sour face.

"Did you three have a nice little chat with Virginia?" she asked in that sickly sweet voice she used right before a violent event came crashing down on us.

"Yes," we said.

"Well, that's good." She cast narrowed glances at us. "I hear you're going to see your mom and dad?"

John nodded and her eyes squinted to the point of being shut totally.

"You remember what happened last time you told lies about us, don't you?"

We stood frozen, not daring to answer. She stood and in a low, mean whisper she hissed, "You'll never see them again if you say one bad thing. Do you understand?"

Standing statue-still, we said nothing.

"Do you understand?" she repeated, leaning forward, inches from us.

We nodded and, just like that, she stood straight up, smiled, and simply said, "Good! Now, there're orders to load out. Get to it, kiddos."

The three of them—father, mother, and fat-ass son—took it easy on us the entire week leading up to our visit with Mom and Dad. Our chore load was reasonable and food intake increased. Whippings were nil, even if we broke one of their golden rules.

Hope graced me. This would be more than a visit. I pictured our mom, sad and crying, painfully listening to our stories of abuse. I could see my dad's neck, corded with muscle, turning red. His large, meaty sledgehammers for hands, balling into fists. His eyebrows would angrily knit themselves closer together with each horrific syllable being relayed.

There was no way he would allow this to continue under his watch. No fucking way. He would put us in the car, take us home, and then turn right around and make a road trip right quick to Ridgeway to kick some ass. These were the thoughts that consumed me the whole week. By the time Saturday arrived and Virginia rolled up the drive, I had convinced myself this scenario would soon play out and I could not wait.

Our road trip began and, after an excited forty-five minutes, we pulled up to a park in a small town unknown to me. Standing there, side by side, were our mom and dad. Virginia could barely stop us from bolting out of the car before it rolled to a stop. I rushed to my hero, my savior, my dad! He scooped me up and hugged me hard and I took in the familiar smell of diesel fuel and asphalt, embedded in the very fibers of every shirt he wore. He set me down, and I jumped over to where my mom stood.

She looked great. Her hair and make-up applied real nice and a large, caring smile lit up her face. This was her. This was the woman I knew and loved. Not the blathering, dark woman I'd last seen before they took us in the middle of the night.

Virginia seated herself at a picnic table right next to the one we were to occupy and eyed the reunion. Our parents had bags of burgers, fries, and sodas waiting for us, and we dug in like ravenous animals.

"Good lord, guys, slow down before one of you chokes," our mom exclaimed.

We began asking about our sisters and Mom said they were being cared for by a real, nice family a short distance from here. Shortly thereafter, a car pulled up and our oldest sister, Jennifer, and our tiny little sister, Julie, came rushing out, the youngest toddling around and not as enthusiastic as the eldest. Jennifer gave each of us a massive hug and then went off to our parents. Everybody seemed to talk over one another a lot.

"I've been playing volleyball and I'm in the 4-H club," Jennifer boasted. She told us her foster mother was teaching her to knit and sew and that riding horses was something she had taken up as well. "How about you?" she directed toward us.

Utter silence replaced the overzealous laughter.

"We've been getting beat," John said.

Dad looked at Mom. She was already looking back at him.

"It's true, we are. I swear to God," Jason said.

"You gotta keep us, Dad," I added my two cents.

Jennifer looked at us with a bit of concern and confusion as if asking, *What the fuck?* She turned her attention to our parents along with us.

Let the full on, unadulterated ass kicking begin. This was what I'd been obsessing over the entire week. The day of reckoning had come. The sins of the Ward family were going to haunt them, tenfold.

My mom dropped her head and stared down at the gaps in the picnic table and my dad, well, he looked over to where our social worker had planted herself.

"Virginia had a talk with us earlier this week, boys."

Okay, good. We're here now. We're safe with you, so go kill them and let's go home, I thought.

He went on.

"Do you think maybe you're over-exaggerating a little, guys?" Dad questioned.

Then John got hot.

"No, Dad! They're killing us!"

Dad gave John the "sit down and calm down" look, and he did, all the while lowering his voice but still pleading with the old man. Virginia sat silent, observing what was unfolding and, just as important, listening to what was being said. Her head up, not interrupting, Mom stared straight forward, that fucking familiar glazed look in her eyes. Our dad was trying, desperately, to diffuse the ticking time bomb in our mother's head.

In a nutshell, the conversation continued with Dad assuring us Virginia had our best interest at heart and would make sure we were alright. We continued spilling our guts as Dad's eyes darted from Mom to Virginia.

"Maybe they're telling the truth, Dad," Jennifer said.

"Enough!" he growled.

His face was now bright red versus deep tan. Mom jumped, looking embarrassed. A small, crooked smile adorned her face.

Well, welcome back, Mom. Great to see you again! Did you have a pleasant trip?

Dad breathed deep and exhaled even longer. "Now you listen to me, right now." He had our attention. "Your mom and I are working hard to get you home and this is not helping."

This was not how it should go, goddammit. Dad was our Superman. He needed to be swooping in, cradling us in his muscular arms, rescuing us in the nick of time. Not folding like a cheap suit under the watchful eye of some lady with a notepad, a pencil, and a fucking polyester pantsuit!

"Virginia will take care of everything, okay?" he finished, looking toward our state-assigned social worker.

Who was this imposter? *What have you done with my dad?* I wanted *that* man, our hero, right now.

Instead, the look on his face said, *See, Virginia? See how I took care of the situation? See how I held my temper and made it all better? Can I have my kids back now? Can I please, Virginia, please?*

The man, larger than life and yet somehow so small, stood and guided Mom from her seated position by the elbow as Virginia motioned to her watch. Our time was up and I knew we were going back to that fucking farm.

"Come with me to the car," he said.

Wait, are we about to make a break for it? Was the old man setting her up? Road trip anyone?

Snake eyes. No such luck.

John and Jason's birthdays in May had come and gone without a second thought from anybody back in Ridgeway. Dad led us to the bed of his truck. Lying in the back was a black-over-green, brand spanking new bicycle for John. Dad pulled it out with one hand and presented it to him.

"Try it out," he said with a wide smile on his face.

John, reluctant at first to obey, rode in circles until our warden cut our time off. Just like that, our time was over. Dad promised Jason he would get his present when we were all home together again. Jennifer and Julie stood by the car that had brought them. Their foster parents hadn't even intruded on our sisters' time with their family. No secrets to hide or a need to skulk around corners in their foster family's case.

We hugged each other hard, not wanting to go. Dad and Mom, who was now back with us in our time zone, assured us of how hard they were working to get us home. Virginia loaded John's bike into the backseat of the small Datsun. Jason and I cried, but John did not. Jason got in the front seat and John and I slid under the wheels and pedals of the bike and away we went, waving until we turned the corner and could no longer see them.

We made it back with plenty of sunshine left in the day, so John took off on his new bike, proud as a peacock. It wasn't long before Robbie showed up and began asking John for a turn on it. As the little prick had done to him, John denied him a ride on his new wheels. Robbie ran to tell on him and, instead of just letting it go, Walter came outside and called John over to where he stood. Then, being the big, fucking prick he was, he had John dismount from his new mode of transportation. He pulled out his pocketknife, flipped the blade out, and made a scratch on one spot of the rack bar and then five inches from that, another identical scratch mark.

He handed John the knife and said, "Scrape all the paint off between the two marks, and I mean every spot of paint or I'll kick your little ass right up between your shoulders." He took in our faces, then finished, "That's what selfish sons of whores get when they don't want to share."

Hesitating, looking down at the gift our parents had just given to him, the only genuine item that was truly his, John reached down and dragged the blade across the shiny, fresh paint. As it flecked away, tears rolled down his face for what would be the last time he would cry while at this place. He would not give them the satisfaction again. It didn't matter how bad they beat or kicked him. Calling our parents every name under the sky would no longer coax the response they craved.

These people were creative with mental and verbal abuse. Boots and belts weren't imaginative, but they were effective from a physical aspect. The verbal jabs they directed toward us? Well, after a while, one, if not all three of us, could have mocked them, word for word, as they spoke the sentences they used to belittle us three brothers and our bloodline. It sticks with you.

CHAPTER TWENTY-THREE

It was another day, another set of overnight gushers, courtesy of Jason and John. The brutal lessons administered down in the pits of hell with Satan took place as always. After the warm, morning breeze began drying overlapping stains on their mattresses under the willow tree, we set upon our chores with Carol's command of "Hop to, kiddos. There's much to do before this afternoon."

We went about at a blistering pace, trying to complete our tasks as fast as possible, but not because it was a special day for any of us. It was because it was Robbie's birthday today. His school-age buddies would arrive early in the afternoon for his birthday party and my brothers, desperate to hide their indiscretions, rushed to finish before a single child could arrive and catch the slightest glimpse of their stained mattresses. I helped them move the stinking beds back down where they belonged, just as Mother Nature had finished her work on them.

"You don't want your school friends to see what you did. That would be embarrassing," Walter said, feigning concern. One would almost believe he actually cared about humiliating us if you didn't know any better.

We had done what we set out to do just in the nick of time. Children ranging from ages eight to ten trickled in for the party, wrapped gifts under one arm and sleeping bags under the other. Some spoke to John and Jason, but not to me. I didn't know any of them and they didn't know me. They all converged on Robbie. The prince had their attention, as it should be. It was his special day, after all. That was just fine with us.

Robbie reveled in the focus. He ushered them around and showed off his prized possessions.

"Look at my motorcycle."

"Look at my wind-up Evel Knievel racer."

He may as well have said, "Look at what I've got and all that I have. I'm loved and adored by many. See all of my friends who've come from far and wide to pay homage to His Highness."

A badminton court went up in the middle of the backyard. Ten children had shown up for the glorious occasion. I didn't take part because I was small and the teams were even at twelve–six on each side of the net. John and Jason, having never played, picked it up pretty quick and were playing well, much to Robbie's dismay. If they hit an excellent shot or recovered fast on another, I'd cheer them on over every "chuh" that escaped Robbie's lips.

Arthur finally pulled me aside and instructed me to keep quiet.

"Nobody wants to hear from the peanut gallery," he scolded, burying his fingertips in my shoulder.

It wasn't my fault Robbie sucked and the two outsiders were getting better by the volley. God forbid someone was to encourage John and Jason. From there on out, I kept quiet and had to stop myself from clapping or jumping up in appreciation with every swing of their rackets that proved fruitful. The boys, other than Robbie, would give a "good job", "nice one", or "groovy shot". Arthur didn't shut them down. He wouldn't want to make an ass out of himself, correcting those he had no control over.

Robbie tired of the game after a short while, be it out of boredom or because of the equal status being given to my brothers.

"Chuh, this game is stupid, chuh," he complained.

Just like that, the fun everyone seemed to enjoy was over.

"Let's keep playing, Robbie, come on," Jason said.

Robbie looked through my brother without responding to him and instead said, "Let's put the tent up over by the garden."

All the boys, minus us, began assembling poles and laying out the ten-man tent bought special for the occasion and, after much arguing and shouting instructions, had it put up, leaving the front-door flaps fluttering in the early evening gusts. In the house, an unenthusiastic, out of tune "Happy Birthday" bounced off the walls. Cake and punch appeared, and we partook in it just like everyone else. We enjoyed the sherbet and lemon-lime soda mixture and chocolate sheet cake, relishing every little sip and each delectable bite. I took my time, knowing moments like these were few. We three would not waste the date, gulping it down.

Gifts were the next order of business. One at a time, and with complete attention being paid to the little prick, Robbie tore through colored paper, coiled ribbon, and affixed bows. Cards wishing him the best day possible? Ignored, right along with whoever could not afford to give a gift. He only had eyes for the shiny new toys he could brag about and wave in our faces.

When the great presentation was over, it was right back outside for hide-and-seek and the familiar, "red rover, red rover, send whomever right over". After running around all evening, with Robbie doing his best to keep the attention off of us and on him, night fell. Boys were now exploring the inside of the large, vinyl structure that would house them for this night. Frank had shown up and built a small fire pit to complete the outdoor ambience. It would have been the perfect opportunity for hot dogs or s'mores, but I guess nobody thought of that—except the kids.

"If we even just had marshmallows, we could roast them on sticks or hangers," one boy said.

"Or franks," said another.

"Hotdogs," one boy corrected. "Frank is my dad's name, numb nuts."

That comment brought about boisterous laughter.

"Franks is a stupid name for a hotdog," the same boy exclaimed. The laughter continued.

Sleeping bags were uncoiled and with spots picked out, the boys gathered around the fire. We broke into groups, some droning on about sports, girls, and hunting until Frank pulled up a fireside seat and told all of us to quiet down and pay attention. Two boys were deep in a heated conversation about who would make it to the Superbowl this year. They'd settled on five: Raiders, Steelers, Cowboys, Falcons, or Chiefs. Another group was concentrating on the upcoming hunting season and whose dad would bag the biggest buck this year.

"I said quiet down and pay attention," Frank demanded.

He paused and his tone took on an ominous, foreboding seriousness, accompanied by an odd look on his face. A few boys murmured a bit longer and Robbie elbowed one of them in the ribs.

"Shush, chuh," he whispered.

"Ow, Robbie, geez, man," the boy said.

"My brother's got something serious to say, chuh," he returned.

"Okay, man, gosh."

The group had now come to a complete standstill. Frank had the stage.

So began the saga of Rufus McGruder.

"You boys have got to understand, you're all taking a tremendous risk just hearing this and an even more unimaginable bet staying out here tonight in that flimsy tent," Frank said. He hooked his thumb toward our temporary sleeping quarters.

I'd be lying if I said that statement didn't perk up a few deaf ears. Every boy, now quiet, honed in on the man with a serious tale to tell, awaiting his next syllable.

"A long time ago, I'd say around a hundred years, a man named Rufus McGruder lived just back behind here, on this very land. Rufus was awful proud of his garden. He grew corn, taters, green beans, peas, and carrots. When time came to harvest, he'd pick the veggies and clean them up real nice-like, place a mess of them in wood baskets, and sell his growings to folks passing by his place. They say he grew the most delicious and sizeable vegetables around here."

Some of us were content to follow the lead up to the story. Others were already turning back to one another to whisper and murmur about other things. Observing the lot of us growing bored, Frank got to the point, voice elevated.

"One night, a group of boys, I'd say your age, snuck up to old Rufus's shack and ransacked his garden, stealing and stomping the entire plot. When the old man awoke and seen what they'd done, he went crazy. Word got back to him which boys had destroyed his money-making crop and he went after them." He stared straight at me, eyes locked-in on mine. "Their folks too," he added.

"What did he do?" Robbie asked. For a few seconds, he looked like a regular kid hanging on his big brother's words.

Frank surveyed the circle, looking us up and down.

"He killed eight all together, two parents and six kids in total." Frank had set the hook. Now all he had to do was reel us in.

"The local law got hold of him. By local law, I mean vigilantes."

"They shot him, didn't they?" Jason asked.

Frank stared back at Jason, unblinking.

"They strung him up, boys. Right up there in that old cemetery."

He pointed past the pasture, up the hill toward the old church.

We've been messing around up there since we arrived and he's springing this shit on us! I thought. *Shit, we've all climbed that big old tree up in the center of the property!*

The group of us sat, staring at one another, amazed at what we had just heard, and then Frank finished his tale.

"You boys are camping out right next to the garden, you realize that, right?"

We looked over toward the Ward family garden. It had always been a pain in the ass for us and now this shit.

"Rufus, he don't cotton to folks messing around near his garden," Frank said.

"That isn't his garden, Frank. It's Mom's, chuh," the little prick pointed out.

"Every garden is his garden, Robbie. He's a ghost, and he doesn't know he's a ghost, but he knows one thing." Frank paused again in the dead silence. "If he sees you young boys out here, tonight, next to his garden, he'll strangle you with his cold, dead hands!"

Scared shitless and being seven years old, he reeled me in and landed me. Falling for this fireside folly from an adult who didn't appear to be bullshitting us had me covered in goosebumps. Frank left us with one small piece of advice.

"If you hear old Rufus McGruder outside the tent, you better stay quiet... and I mean as quiet as a mouse like the ones in that church up on the hill. If he knows you're here, it's over."

With that, Frank stood and said he was going inside to hit the hay, leaving us to our thoughts and spiraling imaginations. Half of us had shifted to the other side of the fire pit, facing uphill, eyes scanning the steepled silhouette hulking in shadow—gravestones, ever-present and dutiful, standing their posts. Some boys called Frank's bullshit right after he left, but I, for one, was not about to take any chances. I planned on sleeping inside that night, well out of Rufus's reach and his miserable garden. As luck would have it, I was told I'd be staying in the great outdoors with everyone else.

Talk returned to sports, and hunting with more girls added to the mix. Walter lumbered down the backstairs and beckoned Jason and John over to where he stood.

"You two come with me," he said to my brothers.

I knew this couldn't be good. Surely, he wouldn't beat the crap out of them in front of, or in earshot of, all these other boys. He directed my brothers inside and down the stairs to what was soon to be one of the fat bastard's crowning moments.

"Follow me, guys. Quick, hurry," Robbie instructed.

He lined his buddies up on the ground around the windows, making sure all there had a ringside view at the circus. When I arrived and peered through one of the skinny windows, I saw my older brothers standing before Walter, removing their shirts. He made them remove their pants and socks. The son of a bitch's jovial, muffled voice seeped through the glass. He spoke loud enough to be heard over the snickering of a few of Robbie's party guests.

"Underwear, too, pissants. Wouldn't want them to get soaked as well."

Horrified, they began taking off the one article of clothing that held their dignity intact. Now, nude and casting momentary glances toward the windows where their peers' faces were now pressed, they covered their genitals and, in shame, averted their eyes toward the ground. My brothers' bodies were skinny and pale with reminders of previous leather lashes and bruises from the bastard's boots, peppering their legs, buttocks, and ribcages.

Tears began filling my eyes, and I wiped at them, ashamed for my brothers and embarrassed to be crying in front of the older group of boys. Lying at Walter's feet were two cloth diapers and four large safety pins. The show went on.

"Raise your arms above your heads," Walter said.

Neither did as told, covering their private parts with both hands, eyes fixated on the cement floor.

"Now!" he yelled.

Upon hearing the elevated volume of his voice, they raised their bony arms skyward, revealing themselves for all to see. The young men, who just moments before had been laughing, now were silent. The only one still laughing was the little prick.

I wondered if their silence meant that they were seeing what I saw. Feeling something close to what I was feeling. Did they realize what was taking place right before their eyes? Were they growing more uncomfortable by the second?

"Keep them up there until I'm finished," Walter ordered.

He reached for one diaper and placed it across John's groin and pushed it through his legs and reached around, pulling one side to his bruised hip.

"Hold still," he said. Then he chuckled. "Wouldn't want to stick you."

Jason, still on full display, glanced up at the windows, met our eyes, then closed his. I continued to cry in silence. When the fat bastard finished diapering my oldest brother, he turned his attention to Jason.

"Keep them hands high, boy."

As he began placing the diaper on Jason, he preached to them.

"We can't have you little pissants getting the other boys wet, can we?"

I turned away and walked to the corner of the house, crying openly. My heart broke for my brothers. Nothing could stop the main event being presented to the spectators by hell's ringmaster in the basement.

Soon, my brothers joined us back outside, dressed and warming themselves by the fire. Nobody, not one boy, including the little prick, said a word about what they'd just witnessed.

We bedded down in the tent and covered up. I cried more into my blankets. I didn't know the word, but I had seen it in totality. The word that my brothers had experienced in its entirety that night was 'humiliation'. I was ashamed and hurt inside. If I felt this way, I cannot imagine how they must have felt. Their dignity and self-respect stripped away and cast to the stagnant, dank air down in that hellhole.

Later that night, Frank, the great storyteller, thought it would be fun to moan and groan and judder the tent, emulating old Rufus. I awoke to complete chaos and began screaming and crying, more than the older boys. Freaking out, Carol removed me from the tent and began beating me from the middle of my back to just above the back of my knees with a fresh strip of baling wire. It hurt like hellfire as she shoved me across the yard to the back door, swinging for the fences the entire way. Blue-

and-purple lines began rising on the posterior of my body, creating a painful, burning road map wherever wire had struck skin. Later in the evening, blood seeped from my wounds, adhering fabric to flesh.

Our summer was ending, and school would soon begin. My backside would heal with time. The torch of humiliation my brothers carried would remain stoked for a lifetime, igniting a burning anger in them.

Like smoldering lint, attaining necessary oxygen, reaching its flash point in a clogged dryer hose.

CHAPTER TWENTY-FOUR

Summer drew to an end, and we were about as demoralized as we had ever been. Beaten down, exhausted both mentally and physically. We'd grown morose and listless, even by our own standards. Routine became almost as comforting as it was dreadful in our collective jaded state. The Wards had to disrupt even that routine. Lord forbid we ever enjoy a modicum of comfort, no matter how warped and twisted.

They dragged us along like unwanted baggage to the swimming hole, better known as Chetopa Creek. I knew Chetopa Creek for lots of things, but for kids my age, it was popular for the rope swing affixed to a large limb hanging low near the water. They had given my brothers and me the strange honor of being present on Walter and Robbie's retreat.

We took turns swinging out as far as we could go. Robbie went first. He balanced on a large root at the base of the tree where someone from summers gone-by had attached it. Robbie slipped his foot through a loop at the bottom. Then, he pushed off with his free foot, all the while holding tight with both hands.

We learned we could then swing out and let go, splashing down closer to the creek bank. The second option was to build momentum, much like one would on a swing set, allowing us to reach the middle of the creek at a higher speed. Robbie splashed down near the jutting edge of earth.

Walter went next, his whale of a body crashing into the water like a literal cannonball. John went next, then Jason, followed by me. We fell into a rhythm where we waited for each other to have their turn. Even Robbie seemed happy to wait for each of us brothers to have our fun. After several turns, Jason stepped up and readied himself on the rope, pushed off, and began the pendulum action necessary to get him to the center. Just as he gave the rope one final, centrifugal push, he attempted to go in backward and his right foot slipped through the loop.

It snared him, just like a rabbit.

His efforts to lift at the waist kept his head from being submerged. At first, all of us in attendance busted a gut laughing. But as he slowed and came to a stop, he could no longer keep his head out of the water for more than a couple of seconds. Zapped of strength, his head went under and stayed submerged, feet and legs kicking. John and I jumped in, but we couldn't touch bottom.

Lack of the pendulum motion stretched the rope tight, leaving Jason kicking like mad now. We took turns trying to raise his head, but when we got him to air, we'd sink and he'd go right back under.

Walter and Robbie were really getting a kick out of the entire ordeal.

"Help! Help, please!" I begged.

Walter continued laughing until Jason's frantic kicking slowed. He jumped in, but by that time, our trapped brother had faded. He was barely moving a muscle. Walter, submerged to his chest, reached Jason and lifted his head out of the water. Jason vomited water down the front of his face, then began gasping. He was clear.

Or so we thought.

Walter let him catch his breath, then the evil bastard dropped him back in the water and the whole kicking ordeal started again. He waited until Jason's body quieted, like a fish resigning itself to its fate suspended in air on the hook. He lifted Jason's head once more. Jason's eyes struggled to remain open. His breathing was ragged and sporadic between bouts of water being expelled out of his mouth. John and I were helpless. We felt as though we were drowning right alongside our brother.

Struggle.

Kick.

Kick slower.

Quit kicking.

Lift and repeat.

The twisted prick did this a couple more times before finally freeing him.

Jason, having gained a burst of life from the reprieve, paddled like the dickens all the way back to the bank while the fat fuck belly-laughed the entire time. Had it been any of us, I believe the same scenario would have played out. I knew the fat ass hated all of us. No need for any more proof. Since I had moved upstairs, I had avoided him more. I still got mine regularly, but it wasn't from him all the time.

Playing that kind of game with our brother, though? That was just sick.

Walter somehow seemed darker and more sadistic than ever.

The incident at the watering hole made me more aware of it. After that day, I realized beatings were getting longer and harder, too. I'd hear him whip my brothers' asses downstairs for five or ten straight minutes after soiling the bed. It wasn't uncommon for one of them to have to peel the underwear from their asses. Blood stains had showed up on their clothing more than it had in the recent past.

Amid Walter's ever-worsening temper, some good news came our way courtesy of a phone call from Virginia. Our mom was doing a lot better and Dad had landed a new job at a coal mine, making more money. Alcohol was no longer part of the equation. He had quit drinking for us, his children. They had done their part and lived up to the court-ordered mandates that would secure our freedom from that hellhole.

But that didn't mean freedom. Not yet.

Instead, we got to go back to school. This was its own retreat from the farm and from Walter's wrath. For eight blissful hours a day, we got to interact with people that operated on basic human decency instead of spiteful anger and sadism.

Yes, things were looking up for us brothers.

But it wouldn't be enough. Never enough.

CHAPTER TWENTY-FIVE

The first few weeks back at school were as uneventful as I had hoped. It reverted to being a haven where I could take a break from the hard labor and sour milk waiting for me back "home". But it also went back to being a place where no one noticed anything or, if they did, said nothing.

The fresh faces in the faculty and student body joined right on in with the rest of the school in letting three beaten-down, hurting boys slip into anonymity. School was a safe place, but it wasn't the place to be saved.

Before we knew it, Thanksgiving was upon us. The foster family celebrated this holiday with gusto and, for once, they didn't leave us out. They and their extended family met at a church hall rented for the occasion and we feasted upon a meal unlike anything we had had since arriving almost a year prior.

Turkey and all the trimmings were bountiful, and they encouraged second helpings. We had more than our fair share. If only Saturday meals could've been the same. We'd have been in pretty decent shape.

But that wasn't the case and even during a joyous occasion like this, we were skinny and rundown. We don't have pictures of us during that time of our lives, but I can only imagine how ghastly we must have appeared to anyone who knew what they were looking for. I remember seeing dark circles painted under my brother's eyes. I remember our cheekbones being quite pronounced, along with our ribcages.

The changes in our bodies had seemed strange to me even then. An adult's perspective should have rung five-alarm fire bells.

On the ride home, an unseasonably strong thunderstorm hit and the wind, rain, and lightning were in full force. We boys rode in Walter's truck. Carol and Arthur had gone ahead with tubs of leftovers they'd secured from the banquet table. We wouldn't be seeing any of it. As Walter traversed the muddy and fast-flooding back roads, the story of Rufus McGruder came up and Walter came to a stop on the dark, deserted road.

"They say old Rufus haunts a big, two-story house close to here," he said.

Robbie chimed in with, "I thought he lived in an old shack? Frank said so."

"He's a ghost now, Robbie. He can live where he wants and travel anyplace in the world."

I had already had a terrible experience involving old Rufus that ended with me screaming and getting tore up with baling wire. I didn't want to hear anything more about him.

"Let's go look at his house. Maybe he'll look out a window," an enthusiastic Robbie demanded.

Walter drove to the next mile section and turned left and went a few mile sections. Overgrown and dying bushes crowded the opening to the driveway as Walter nosed through. The headlights fell upon an abandoned, run-down house. It was a two-story river rock facade with two large columns holding up the dilapidated overhang. The front door banged open and shut in the wind and someone had busted all the windows out.

"Who's going in first?" Walter asked.

"Chuh, no way, Walter."

My brothers and I remained silent. I tried to bury myself behind them so he wouldn't ask me to go.

"Joseph, you'll go first."

It was dumb of me to forget that Walter didn't ask; he told and, when he did, we had better be hopping to it. I started crying as the wind and lightning picked up. The rain had let up some, but howling wind and thunderous lightning? Pair that with a haunted house? In my mind, a ghost who wasn't fond of kids just might take issue with a young man busting into his place.

It terrified me.

"Go!" Walter yelled.

"Please, Walter, don't make me go in there."

He glared at me in the rearview mirror. His gut was too big for him to turn around in his seat.

The glorious meal I had just consumed turned to thick cement in my stomach.

"One, two, three..."

Oh shit, he's counting like Carol!

Now, I knew what sort of hurt to expect when the counting started if I didn't get a move on, so through my tears, I opened the back car door and stepped out.

"You better move or I'm leaving you here, boy."

I mustered all the courage I could and ran, full sprint, to the house. I got to the door and turned back. He called out the driver's side window, "You have to go in!"

Scared as hell, I slunk back toward the door. Just as I jumped over the threshold, the headlights from the car joggled. I whipped back around and in horror realized Walter was backing out at a high rate of speed.

"Wait!" I screamed in terror.

I ran back toward the car. By this time, the nose was facing down the road and I was running in the dark. The rain was kicking up hard again. Muddy gravel and soupy filth splattered me as he peeled away, ruby-red taillights growing smaller by the second.

Robbie, John, and Jason peered back through the rear window. Their alabaster faces went out like an old picture tube on a television. I stood, icy rain soaking every inch of me. My one source of light was the electrified, black sky.

Running after them in the dark was not an option. What if I got lost and they couldn't find me? I ran back to the house and stood crying on the porch, praying headlights would soon pull through the opening, rescuing me from Rufus and the elements.

Rain fell at an angle because of high winds and, as luck would have it, smack-dab in my face. I had two choices: stay out here, braving the wind, rain, and lightning, or step back through the banging door and keep watch from inside for them to return. With any luck, there would be no showdown with my imagination and the ethereal old Rufus.

I was shivering now and soaked clean through. I opted for the latter and eased through the doorway, trembling from the chilly deluge and mind-bending fear, scared as hell.

I looked around as the night sky lit the interior of the old house. I saw in the gloom a stone fireplace and then darkness again. A second flash revealed an old chair in a corner. Again blackness. The good news was, for the time being, there was no sign of Rufus.

I positioned myself to the right of the handle-side of the door, peeking toward the drive about every five seconds.

Surely they would come back soon. They wouldn't leave me out here all night?

After some passage of time, I found the courage to crawl into a corner. I felt like a deer during hunting season. Senses at maximum. Tasting and smelling the metallic, moldy environment. Praying each palpation of the fingers met scored, solid wood, anticipating every skittering, whistling, wind-driven echo. Old Rufus had to be watching me. His eyes were convicting me. Every time the night sky erupted with electricity, my own eyes betrayed me. Leaving behind midair negatives of the last thing I saw each time I'd blink.

Would he leave me alone, entertained enough by my timid fumbling in the dark to let me live? In my circuits around the interior of the house, I'd brushed up against old rickety furniture and overgrown weeds that had made their way inside. But every so often, I felt something that I couldn't quite identify.

Was it a hand? Was it Rufus reaching out to trip me up or skeletal remains of one of his previous victims?

My legs locked up, and I curled into a corner, watching the play of lightning as it flashed against the walls. I waited in a numb sort of daze next to a pile of puke, having lost my meal. So, I watched and waited for my death or for Walter to turn around and save me. My brain had gone past the point of thinking about what could and should happen. It had latched onto one thought only.

They can't leave me here all night.

Turned out they could and, by God, they did. The bastards left me there.

After the terror had lost its novelty, exhaustion set in. I would doze off, my head lolling back against the corner I had backed myself in, then jolt awake with each crash of thunder. Heart racing again, I would look around, imagining all the ways this would be the end. Rufus would strike at any moment. The wind would send the old house crashing down around me. The lightning would set the place ablaze with me trapped inside. Exhaustion would overtake me again and I would list to the side. Something else would shock me awake, then it was back to imagining the many ways this night would be my last.

By the time Walter retrieved me the next morning, just as the sun was rising, I was half-frozen from being wet all night. I didn't feel it, though. I looked upon the world around me as Walter frog-marched me to the waiting car. It all seemed so surreal and calm, as if they had transported the landscape from a different dimension and plopped it down right there.

A dim, powdery sky had overtaken the storm. Barren branches no longer taunted me. They were just shadows dancing on the walls of the home.

I never saw Rufus.

As we walked to the truck, Walter said, "I'll bet you won't fear tall tales about ghosts again, you little pussy."

I climbed into his truck.

"Did you hear what I said? He's not real. It's just a made-up story."

Freezing and tired, I finally responded, "Why didn't you just tell me it wasn't real?"

The fat bastard, in his warped way of thinking, said, "You wouldn't have learned anything."

I said nothing else, and neither did he. We just stared out the windows at the passing landscape. I'd like to think that maybe he realized what he did, and what his parents allowed, had gone too far. Upon arriving back at the house, neither parent checked on me. Nobody offered an apology or a fucking blanket.

Going far for one person can be different for some people. Getting on an airplane for the first time because of a fear of flying is pushing the limit for some, while jumping out of a perfectly good airplane seems logical for others. If Walter had his way, he'd have been in charge of shoving a person, scared to death of heights, out of the plane without a parachute, screaming lessons from the door as his pupil plummeted to the earth.

"Don't be scared, pussy! Aim for the haystack and you'll be fine!"

Walter wasn't an excellent teacher, but a lesson is a lesson. It wasn't the one that Walter had intended, but I had learned something all the same. John and Jason, I realized, had learned a similar lesson long before I had.

That piece of shit in the basement. He had repeatedly proved himself to be rotten, evil to the core. Had he been born that way? I think not. Had he been groomed to be evil? Was any morality he had been born with secondary to his own upbringing? Maybe lessons passed down from parent to child truly did stick. Or, in Walter's case, maybe they grew and evolved.

There had been plenty of children before us to practice on. Plenty.

How do you get to Carnegie Hall?

Practice.

CHAPTER TWENTY-SIX

"I was downstairs when it happened," John begins.

"Jason had pissed the bed again, like so many times before. Walter was in a terrible mood, if you can remember, from the night before. Who knows why, he just was."

John's eyes are off in the distance, just over my shoulder, remembering. The weight of Sheriff Luxemberg's presence is heavy on the other side of the door, listening in on his microphone, watching on a closed-circuit camera.

I remember. The night before, Walter had returned, exhibiting a dark and hateful frame of mind.

"Get the hell out of my way, you little fuckers," he'd growled before climbing the few steps to the back door. Perhaps it had been a bad day at work. Maybe the gal we suspected he'd been hanging out with had been on the rag and had been eating on his ass. Who knows? All I know is that Walter had been in a bad mood. Nothing good happened when he was in the shits.

"He woke up the next morning, walked through that door, and jerked Jason from the bed and, lo-and-behold, a stain. Walter seemed really pleased. He was looking for something to punish us for. Not like he needed a reason, but it made him feel better. He pulled me out next, but

I was dry. I crawled back on my bed while he grabbed a fistful of Jason's hair and threw him across the floor.

"He hit his head pretty good when he slid across the concrete. It dazed him some, but he was awake–foggy, but awake. When Walter reached him, he was propping himself up on his elbows. He kicked him in the ribs. It was a heck of a shot, hard enough to spin his body to where he was facing me instead of the stairs."

I remember waking up to the all too familiar sounds of one of my brothers getting tore up downstairs.

"You sinner! You little fucker!"

I recall thinking his lungs were working overtime that morning. Some days, I never knew when he'd punished one of my brothers until I saw them or noticed a mattress against the house or the weeping willow tree. I'd learned to live with it. The house shook from the shouting and Robbie had grumbled aloud, rousing him from his sleep.

I can't wait to go home, I remember thinking to myself, rolling over and out of bed.

John continues.

"Walter went to kick again and Jason rolled right. Walter missed and almost fell on his fat ass. If he would have lost his balance and hit his head on the washing machine, maybe–"

John swallows. His throat seems dry. I think about asking for a glass of water.

"That pissed the fucker off even more. I didn't think it was possible to make him madder, but it did. He was fucking furious."

John's eyes roll upward in thought. He looks back at me, just a miniscule, brief twitch of the muscles in his eyeballs. Suddenly, he seems trapped in memory, and the crazy bastard is dragging me down right along with him.

"While the piece of shit was regaining his balance and searching the floor for our brother, Jason was crawling toward the beds, toward me. Walter is closing in on him and our brother reaches out to me for help and just says, 'John'. Not you, not mom, not dad, not even God. He says 'John'.

"I'm thinking maybe I can call for help. The poor bastards upstairs have never cared before, but they don't want to get caught. I'm thinking I can get them to see that Walter's different this time, that he's going too far. I'm thinking I can call out and get the fucker's attention on me and away from Jason."

John's voice cracks. His face says it all.

"The heel of the prick's boot comes down right on the small of Jason's back. His head drops and that fat fuck takes one step forward and brings the same heel down on the base of his neck."

John's haunted and again, for the second time tonight, not here with me.

"I heard the snap. You ever hear someone's neck break, Joseph?"

I know the question is rhetorical. The part of my higher brain functions that thrives on making snarky remarks to rhetorical questions is short circuiting. The worst part about all of this is that I can't call him a liar.

"You get the fuck up, right fucking now!"

I remember hearing Walter screaming down in the basement. I remember thinking, *Jesus, he's pissed.*

I remember the sound of muffled bootheels on wooden stairs, the banging of the back door and thinking, *Great. The kids on the bus are going to see the mattress and laugh at us, as usual. Why can't they quit pissing the bed, man?* I remember wondering if they knew just how embarrassed I was every time it happened. After all, I was the youngest and all the whispers and finger-pointing found its way to me. One boy on the bus, looking straight at me, had said, "He wet the bed. There's his mattress again. My dad says that's what happens when you play with matches." Little giggles from boys and girls alike had accompanied his quip. The more I thought about it as I got dressed that day, the hotter my face grew. It wasn't just John who felt burdened. Occasionally, I resented them too.

Bare feet rushed down the hall, past my bedroom door. Another pair of slippers followed, running back up the hall and out to the back. I'd finished throwing on my clothes and gone to piss, walking into an empty kitchen. I'd looked out the back door expecting to see wilted, wet mattresses against the willow tree. There was nothing there.

Good. It's against the house, away from prying eyes.

When I had turned to head back to the kitchen, John was sitting on the foot of the stairs, staring up at me.

"Did he pee?" I remember asking.

John said nothing. He just sat there, staring at me, a ghost in gloom.

"Did you pee, John?"

The John back then had nothing to say. The John in front of me now, sitting behind bars, can't say enough.

"When I married, and we had Emily, she couldn't get enough freezer pops. She loved freezer pops. You know, the long ones that come in different colors? Well, Hannah didn't allow her a lot of sugar, being a health nut and all. She used to ask Em what flavor she wanted and after sorting through her choices, she'd always pick red. Hannah would grab that red fucking freezer pop and break it in half, right in the center.

"When you're at home, in your comfy fucking house, Joseph, go grab one out of your freezer and do what Hannah always did. Try it. Then you'll know what it sounded like when Jason's neck snapped.

"He was dead before that mother-fucking fat ass caught his breath."

My chest heaves. Tears fall from my eyes, all the while hoping but knowing that isn't the end.

"Do you remember what I did next, Joseph?"

"No," I whisper. John continues.

"I'll tell you what I did, little brother. Ran to our brother's piss-soaked mattress and hid behind a layer of blankets, pressed my back as hard as I could against the cinderblock wall and pushed my ass as deep into the mattress as it would go. I watched the blood trickle out of his nose and mouth. I watched that piece of shit scoop him up and haul ass up the stairs and out the door with our brother, as limp as a rag doll. When the back door slammed, I ran to the basement window and watched.

"The bastard made his way to the back fence and throws Jason over it like a bag of garbage, like trash thrown to the curb for a truck to smash and dump at a landfill. He heads back to the house, and I hid under the bed, thinking he's coming for me. Instead, he makes his way through the house and gets Arthur and Carol. They run out to the fence and talk for a bit, and then Arthur comes in and lays down the law.

"'Say a word about what happened with Jason, I'll kill you. I'll kill you, I'll kill your family, right down to your sisters.'"

I remember how the back door had flung open and Arthur had rushed right up to me, leaned down, and said, "Go to your room, right now."

He had meant business. I could tell by the speed he walked and the tone of his voice. It was higher than I'd ever heard him speak. I turned and made my way to the room as Arthur descended the stairs and started in on John. "Listen to me, you little bastard..." I caught as I exited earshot. My guess at the time? John had been guilty, and Walter was on Jason, so Arthur was going to be the one that threw down on my older brother.

I remember I thought, *Please let John's mattress be by Jason's, not by the tree*.

I remember I made it to the bedroom. Robbie was sleeping peacefully through it all, not a care or a scare in the world, per usual. I sat on the edge of the bed, waiting to start chores. That's when I heard a car enter the driveway. I got up and peeked out in time to catch the back end of a police car clearing the corner of the house and disappearing toward the backyard. At seven years old, curiosity can get to a young man awful easy. I waited until I heard the cop's car door close and then, against better judgement, snuck down the hall and toward the living room. Hearing voices coming from outside, but unable to understand what was being said, I crept toward the kitchen just as the back door opened again. I stopped in my tracks and dropped to all fours and hid behind the recliner in the corner. Distant sirens cut the morning air.

Arthur's voice drifted my way. "I talked to him, Carol, and he knows better. I can tell you that much."

In a shrill voice, Carol responded, "Oh, sure, like that matters. The little bastards are going home soon and what then, Arthur?"

"Domino did a number on him. It was an *accident*." He emphasized the word 'accident', but the thing set off a small alarm in my head. Even a child can tell when a word spoken in a different tone, stressed more than any other comprising a sentence, means someone's trying to pull a fast one.

"Are you sure?" she asked, pleading.

"I'm sure. Now get out there and put on your best face. Understand, woman?"

She replied with a half-hearted "alright" and they went back outside. I made my way back to the bedroom and continued looking out the window. A white ambulance, similar to the one that took my mother away, was speeding down the road and pulling into the back. I knew then that something was for sure seriously wrong with one of my brothers and, having already seen John, I knew it was Jason. It had to be Jason. Or maybe the fat bastard had had a heart attack in the middle of laying down his punishment. That would have been poetic justice.

Robbie woke up and looked around, realizing he had overslept. "Why didn't anyone wake me up? Chuh. What's going on outside?"

"I don't know. Your mom and dad said for me to stay in here," I said.

He rubbed his eyes and said, "Maybe you have to, but I don't."

He slid out of bed and left the room just as Frank was pulling up to the house. Minutes later, Robbie returned, visibly trembling, and started throwing on clothes about as fast as I'd ever seen his spoiled rotten ass move. He left, and a minute later, Frank was backing out, Robbie in the backseat. Going to school, I assumed.

Looking at Robbie's wall clock and being able to tell time, thanks to Carol, I knew it was going on eight in the morning. I watched the minute hand tick forward.

7:30... 7:35... 7:48...

Finally, Carol, looking disheveled as hell, came in and asked me in that sickly sweet tone of hers to come to the living room. Both emergency vehicles exited the drive and lit their sirens on full blast as they sped away from the house. Carol touched my shoulder as I passed by her and I flinched, not expecting the gentleness of it. Making my way down the hall, I heard Arthur.

"And you damn well better believe I can, buddy boy."

I turned the corner. He was leaning over backward, away from John's face.

"Come. Sit. Now," he said to me.

Doing as I was told, I made my way over to John and sat next to him, only for Arthur to tell him to "go downstairs, right now."

John scooted closer to me instead of following the directions given to him.

"Don't test me, boy."

It was the most menacing tone I'd ever heard from Arthur's mouth.

John stood, head down, and moped through the dining room and out of sight.

Arthur turned his attention toward me. "Your brother, Jason, had an accident this morning."

Now, I had learned that the Ward family was prone to dramatics. But something about the way they were acting today made a chill go down my spine. Before I had an opportunity to ask questions, Arthur spoke.

"Your brother woke early before anyone else and took it upon himself to go outside. Walter got up and immediately noticed he wasn't in his bed, so he went looking for him and, well..." He paused.

"He walked out back and started calling for your brother with no answer and it was only then that he saw him on the other side of the back pasture fence, not moving."

"Is he okay, now?" I couldn't bring myself to think about the emergency vehicles that had already pulled out. I couldn't think about the grim set of every face I had seen that morning. Walter had just been beating on someone down in the basement. He couldn't have had time to go outside and find Jason. But mix one lie in with the truths and it's hard to untangle.

By the time the rest of the empty reassurances that Jason was okay shattered, the lingering doubts that might have led to something more had gone down the drain with them, misappropriated as falsehood by association.

Carol threw a sideways glance at Walter. "We don't know yet. He wasn't breathing when the ambulance took off."

Arthur took over again. "He climbed the back fence and got too close to Domino and he mauled him something fierce."

His eyes were boring holes in the floor when he conveyed this last bit of information to me. Looking back now, I realize that even a piece of shit like the patriarch of this god-forsaken family had trouble stomaching the lie he was spouting.

The room was silent, save for the sound of the clock's pendulum swinging back and forth, but even that was a faint echo. The blood in my ears pulsed with each beat of my heart, drowning out each tick.

"I'm so sorry," Carol said. She seemed genuine.

"But I heard him this morning, yelling at him really loud," I said, pointing at Walter.

The fat bastard shifted his weight and pushed his glasses up the bridge of his sweaty nose and looked at his father.

"John had an accident in bed and Walter was spanking him for it when he noticed your brother was missing."

It would be just like the fat bastard to take so long to notice that

Jason wasn't there, John sleeping right next to him. My thoughts were reeling, trying to take in the information I was just given. I was in a shocked state of mind. This kind of news wasn't something easily processed by a brother, let alone a child.

I was trying to piece things together in a brief span of time, as if I had the right puzzle pieces, but was trying to force the cardboard tabs into the first openings I saw instead of taking the time to find the right ones. The image I was creating just wouldn't match up. If he had been kicking John's ass, he would have noticed Jason's absence because he would have checked his bed as well. That way, he could have doubled his pleasure with a double ass kicking.

He'd pulled that number more times than we could count, that was for sure. But he had been in a funky mood. It could've evolved into "first come first serve" come morning.

Did Jason ever do shit that could have gotten him in a bind? You bet he did. I remember that, frequently when back home, if we wanted a candy bar, we would walk a block and a half to the local food market. I'd wait outside while Jason strolled in as though he were there to shop for a week's worth of groceries, only to emerge with a half-dozen assorted candy bars poking out of his pockets. His greatest caper had been the year prior to being sent to the Wards'. It had been close to the holiday season. We had made it to the food mart, ideas of what he should get floating between us. He had come back out around twenty minutes later, pushing a grocery cart filled with chunks of milk chocolate, cling-wrapped and adorned with gold oval stickers.

"Just walk normal," he'd said to me.

He could tell by the mile-wide smile plastered across my face that I was going to draw unwanted attention. I had stilled myself and, after a block of pushing the squeaky cart down the sidewalk, had asked, utterly astounded, "How did you do that?"

Almost matter of fact, he'd said, "It was just sitting there, so I acted like it was mine and followed other people out."

We ate ourselves sick for half the day until the school custodian had found the cart braced on the stairs that led to the school cellar. Jason had also been the first one of us to stack a couple of mattresses on the ground outside the second-story window of the Mansion and fearlessly fling himself from the opening, landing harmlessly on the cushioned padding below.

So Jason had a history of being quite brazen when an opportunity presented itself or an adrenaline-filled idea struck him just right. It wouldn't have been unlike him to see how close he could get to Domino, the big bastard, or even see if he could outrun him back to the fence. As much as I wanted it not to be true, the story as they presented it made more and more sense. And the police had come and gone without raising a stink over something foul. They would have known if something was wrong. That was their job, after all.

CHAPTER TWENTY-SEVEN

The foster parents retrieved John from the basement, taking turns sitting with us, awaiting any news about our brother. Little to no conversation happened over the next couple of hours. Sometimes, someone would mutter, "I hope he's okay" or "He was foolish to jump the fence with that animal. He knew what a bad temper Domino has." The phone rang twice while we waited. A deputy pulled Walter and Arthur aside twice to talk about the incident. The policeman was still there when Virginia appeared at the front door, knocking lightly.

"How are you boys?" she muttered.

I looked at John, but he didn't seem to be in the mood to be part of the conversation. "We're okay. I'm just wondering about Jason. Do you know anything yet?"

The deputy and Walter joined us in the living room, along with everybody else. They all looked at Virginia like she had the answers to the universe in her polyester back pocket.

"Come here, boys," she said. Her mouth was thin. Her voice sounded odd.

We got up and shuffled over to where she was. She knelt down on one knee.

"Your brother didn't make it."

I couldn't say now how she said it. As cool as a cucumber, like she was commenting on the weather? Maybe she was crying. Perhaps she was whispering. She could've screamed it in our faces. I don't remember. I just know how it made me feel. Like it had jettisoned me down a long, dark tunnel with just enough stale air to avoid suffocation.

I saw spots before my eyes. Tiny, dancing silver sparklers. I would have fallen to the floor had it not been for her wrapping herself around us in an over-perfumed bear hug. It overwhelmed me with the cheap smell of smashed dandelion and sour sweat. I tried to steady myself on trembling knees.

John pulled away from her and shouted, "No!"

Through bleary eyes, I watched him run toward Walter, hands outstretched and balled into little fists. The deputy stepped in front of him before he reached his target while Walter stood back and glared at him for having the audacity to come after him.

"Don't stop him. Let him go and we'll just see what happens," he sneered from behind the officer.

John struggled to free his arms from the policeman's grip without success. Walter was just two feet away from him, his fingers on his belt buckle.

"You killed him, you fat fuck!" he spat. His anger had contorted his face into something ugly that I had never seen on my brother's face before.

I couldn't believe what I was seeing or hearing from John. Didn't he realize what that man was going to do to him?

Virginia hefted herself up and scurried to John and wrapped her arms around his shoulders. When the cop let him go, he spun around and, as hateful as you please, said to her, "Don't you touch me, bitch. This is your fault."

"It was an accident, sweetie," she said.

"We told you what they were doing to us and you did nothing. You left us to fucking *die*!"

"Stop, John, it was an accident," I said.

"Shut up, Joseph. You don't know shit."

John looked at the deputy and said, "Arrest him." Pointing at Walter. "Arrest him. He did it. He killed Jason. The bastard killed him!"

The deputy looked back and forth between the foster family members. "I think he's in shock," he said to nobody.

John quit struggling and Virginia turned loose of him. He went to the front door, opened it, and walked out to the front yard and plopped down on the lawn.

I sat on the couch as the deputy and the family began explaining what had happened in more detail to Virginia.

"It was an unfortunate accident."

"He climbed the fence and tested that darn bull."

"We were asleep. There was nothing we could do."

Walter told his side of the story within my hearing for the first time. "When I found him, I tried. I tried as best as I could to help him, but Domino had done his damage," he said. "It was too late."

"He had half-moon crescents from the bull's hooves and God knows what his insides look like," Arthur said.

I felt faint again. In my brief life, not once had the thought of my brothers' muscles, bones, or guts crossed my mind. Now, to think of them smashed, busted open, or bleeding made my stomach flop like I'd just consumed my daily dose of soured milk. Virginia turned to me.

"Go outside and sit with your brother. He needs you now. Okay?" she said.

I pulled in a deep breath and made my way to the door.

The last words I would ever hear from Arthur were, "He wasn't the brightest bulb of the three, but I never expected he'd do something this stupid."

Carol and Walter nodded in agreement as I made my way out the front door.

John turned to me as I approached and said, "Go away, traitor."

He wouldn't lift his head to look at me. I figured he was crying, so I started crying again as I sat beside him. He flung his left elbow into my ribs.

"Go away!"

It hurt like hell, but I remained where I was, guarding the right side of my body. I leaned forward, inspecting his face for tears. His eyes were dry.

How can he not be crying? I thought. *We just lost our brother, and he's just sitting here, pissed off at the world instead of grieving like a normal human being.*

I scooted down the slope of the yard and turned around, facing him.

"They said it was an accident. Even the policeman said so, John."

"You believe them over me, dumbass?"

"He's a policeman. They don't lie, John."

"Believe what you want. I know what I saw. I know what happened and they're fucking liars."

Maybe it was just like what they had told us, and he was in shock. I had always associated the word 'shock' with what happened when you put a butter knife in an electrical outlet or were forced to piss on an electrified fence, so I figured the news had thrown him for a loop, and he wasn't in the right frame of mind.

"Maybe you were dreaming, John?"

John looked up, and I knew he believed what he thought he had seen. He wasn't crying. He was good and pissed.

Later, Virginia emerged from the house, followed by Arthur, carrying what little belongings we had under both arms in garbage bags. She called us over, but only I walked to where they stood.

"Say goodbye to Carol and Arthur. You're going home."

The overdue joy and relief that should have come from those words didn't come. Jason wasn't there beside us getting to hear those words. Jason's ghost was still down in that nasty basement, waiting to be cast out. I wanted to go back into the house to get him, to reassure him that everything was going to be okay now. As much as I wanted to get away from this place, I didn't want to leave. Jason was here. He was going to come out that door any minute. We had to be waiting for him so we could all go home together.

Virginia walked to where John sat, back to the rest of us. Carol stretched out her arms and I stepped forward into them. She gave me a big hug while Arthur rubbed the top of my head. Walter stepped forward and hugged me and said, "Take care." Then he walked up to the house. It was like the fat fuck just had to have the last word.

"Be good, Joseph. You're a good boy," Carol said.

I walked toward the car. Virginia and John were already waiting on me, with the back door open for me to climb in. John followed me in, shut the door, and hand-cranked the window open.

We rolled backward onto the gravel road. Framed by the window, the foster parents stood on the walkway and Walter stood up on the porch by the front door, looking ahead. Instead, he put his thumb to his throat, dragging it in a left-to-right motion, smirking at John. Virginia, looking forward and driving, was not witness to it.

John's arm shot out the window and his middle finger shot straight up in the air, in full view of Walter's angry, widening eyes. Walter yelled something, red-faced and hopping mad, but his parents turned toward him and started trying to calm him down.

We pulled a right, passing the cemetery, stones at full attention and with Rufus's hanging tree shading them. I looked past John, one last time toward the foster home that had been our hell for over a year, relieved and sorrowful all at once. Life, and John, without our middle brother, would never be the same.

When we arrived back in our hometown, it was back to the boys' home for a few days, not yet being reunited with our parents. John told every adult and child in the place that would listen to him just how our brother's death wasn't an accident... how he was murdered by a demon. He even got into a couple scrapes with a kid that called him "an attention-getter". John promptly made him eat his words.

After a few days, Dad showed up at the boys' home to pick us up. There were big hugs all around and even more when we got home to our sister and mom. John started in with his version about Jason's accident, but Dad shut him down so as not to upset Mom and throw her off the deep end again.

"No second chances next time, boys," he said. "If they come for you again, you won't be coming back until you're grown, understand?"

John walked toward his new bedroom in the rental house. "You were supposed to protect us," he said as he turned his back, breaking Dad's heart for the first, but not the last, time.

After that, my older brother secluded himself away from most of us.

He was always getting into some sort of scrape with local boys or local law enforcement. When he was fifteen, he got arrested for the first time for being a minor in possession. Suspensions and fights in school became normal. His teenage years were the textbook definition of spiraling into juvenile delinquency.

Then, when he was seventeen, he left for the army. Dad had to sign a waiver for him to be eligible to enlist, which he did. John was out of control, and he thought maybe the discipline would do him good. He finished basic training with flying colors. But when he went to his permanent duty station in Germany, he got in a world of hurt for fighting and received a general discharge when he was nineteen.

He came home, got in more scrapes and abused alcohol as though prohibition was just around the corner. Then, when he was twenty-one, he met his wife, Hannah. She changed him some and helped him find religion. They divorced after ten years of marriage when she found another man with more money in his pockets and more religion in his heart than John.

When he was thirty-two, John started taking Xanax for what he said was panic attacks. I think it was to numb his soul and quiet his conscience for failing to protect us. There had been no way to protect us from those people. They were being paid to use us as cheap labor and get their kicks by beating the shit out of three little boys, killing one.

Then, at thirty-six, John slayed the demon that had haunted us our entire lives and landed himself in this cell. Piper paid.

Or, I wish he had.

In truth, John never went and put a shell in Walter's fat face. And Jason never perished in that god-forsaken basement when we were youngsters. But some part of me wishes that had been the case. Maybe, if Jason had expired when we were children, he could have stayed innocent in a way only childhood, no matter how harsh, can afford. Maybe, if he had, he wouldn't have died a slow death of the soul the way John did, walking around now as a grown man with a haunted, inexorable look in his eyes that shows him things I can't see. Walter really went far, almost too far, that damnable day. The Jason I had known and loved as a young man had died, if only in spirit. But the person the experience left behind hurt more to look at sometimes than a stone-cold grave might not.

Part of me wishes, too, that John gave in and got revenge on the family that had forged such a burnt brand on our lives. I looked up their names once a while back. Carol and Arthur live in that same old house. I wonder sometimes if our stained mattresses remain stacked up in the basement somewhere. Walter didn't move far away from the nest, either. Imagine, our greatest torment and our biggest tormentors, still living the good life in the same spot that we'd left them. It wouldn't take much to track them down, to demand retribution, to force out an apology, or to just scream in their faces.

But, somehow, my brothers and I have exercised restraint and, to this day, the Wards remain unbothered by our presence, no matter how I might fantasize otherwise in my darkest moments.

Maybe, just maybe, if John really made that drive—maybe if he pulled the trigger and sent that demon to hell where he belongs, our wounded hearts might settle. Maybe, if John got arrested and sat before me in a jail cell, a ward of the state for yet another time in his life, he could look at me with clear eyes and ask, "Hey, Joseph, do you see ghosts?"

I could stare back at him and respond, "No. Do you?"

Maybe... just maybe, for the first time in our lives, my big brother could look at me with an unburdened smile and answer, "Not anymore."

A BROTHER'S GIFT

E veryone wants a happy ending. Sometimes you get them. Other times? Well...

JOHN

When I began writing this book, my oldest brother had, in recent years, loaded a twelve gauge and sat in his running truck. He had put it in reverse and started backing down the drive. He had hit the brakes, thrown it in gear, and pulled back up to the apartment we shared in our twenties. Then he had left for Kansas City. Without someone who'd been there with him and understood him... would he have done something he'd never be able to take back?

"I swear to God, Joseph. I was close to doing it this time. Too damn close."

He had called from up north and continued to tell me what was on his mind and what he'd like to do. The scenario perfect, scripted in his head.

John said, most nights, it was on a loop up in the old noggin. Placing his head on a pillow, he'd close his eyes and the credits would roll. Teeth grinding, heart racing. A farmhouse in the Midwest, terrified screams, and blood soaking into wallpaper. That's when clenched teeth would relax and a runaway heart would slow.

I made a deal with my older brother. If I write it, will you forget it? We bargained and argued for years. So many nights I'd look at my phone, dreading his number on caller I.D. I mean, he drove me bananas. The guy can get under your skin, no doubt about it. But if it wasn't for him, I would have gotten my ass kicked at the Wards' more times than I care to think about. He took most of the lumps for us. So, I gave him something he wanted: Revenge. Better on paper than real life. He was my great protector. My light in the dark. As I write, he hasn't read one line of this manuscript, but he knows per our agreement, it's over.

So, John. Thank you. No more ghosts. Rest well.

JASON

I received a call at two in the morning in May of 2019. The man on the other end of the line was crying. I mean to tell you, he was bawling like a child. A few minutes passed and I still couldn't make out a single word or phrase he was attempting to say.

"Calm down, man. Take some deep breaths and speak slow," I said.

"I can smell it, Joseph. I can see Walter in the room, and I can smell that goddamn basement."

It took the better part of an hour to get him under control. He said he couldn't believe this was happening. Still haunted by what took place there, he cried, "It should never happen to any children, ever. And it damn sure should not have happened to me or John."

The call was from Jason.

Yes. He's alive and still kicking. I didn't think by the time I finished this book that he would be. Jason has dealt with our past but taken a different road than John or I. Jason drinks to numb what happened. First it was pills, then liquor.

Only three months ago, he had a psychotic episode secondary to alcohol consumption. He'd downed two forty-four-ounce cups of the cheapest vodka you could buy. It nearly killed him. Seeing him in Intensive Care with a tube snaked down his throat for a week broke our hearts.

When asked why he did that to himself, he stated it was because it numbed him, took away the pain and made him feel better. Jason stated he wished he'd died in that basement, rather than live with the torment.

And just as I'd offered to John, I laid out the same proposal.

"Do you want me to kill you off, back in that goddamn basement?"

He took a moment. "Do you think it would help?" he asked.

I told him I couldn't answer that for him. But if it's what he wants, then that's what I'll do.

He went quiet, no more tears and said, "I'd love that."

So, by deciding to allow John to fulfill the revenge that had consumed him... By proposing to Jason that dying in print, rather in life, could kill the past and prove to him life wins and is better, perhaps it would help the two of them.

I'm proud to say he recovered. Jason attended rehabilitation for addiction and no longer couch surfs. He's gainfully employed again and getting back on track.

This is a gift. A gift from me to you two, my brothers. When you read this book, if you do, please know that I remember too, every day. One, my protector. The other, my sidekick.

I love you, my fellow brothers of the state.

Your little brother,
Joseph, June 2022

ABOUT THE AUTHOR

Darrell Lacey was born and raised in Pittsburg, Kansas. He is a U.S. Army veteran who was stationed at Ft. Bragg, North Carolina and served one year in South Korea.

Brothers of the State is Darrell's debut novel. He wrote it based on his own childhood experiences with his brothers. He wrote it during his down time at work over the course of three years. He hopes that his story, while an older one, will shed light on the abuses that have taken place in the foster care system. He also hopes that it will show those that have been through similar situations that there is hope, and that these experiences don't define you.

Darrell hopes to use this book as an opportunity to take classes and continue his education. He is currently working on writing his next novel and a compilation of short stories.

 facebook.com/authordarrelllacey88

 instagram.com/authordarrelllacey88